A
JEWISH
RESPONSE TO
CULTS

EDITED BY

Gary Bretton-Granatoor

UAHC PRESS

NEW YORK, NEW YORK

Library of Congress Cataloging-in-Publication Data

A Jewish response to cults / edited by Gary Bretton-Granatoor.
    p. cm.
  Includes bibliographical references.
  ISBN 0–8074–0604–X (pbk. : alk. paper)
  1. Judaism—Relations. 2. Cults. 3. Judaism—Apologetic works.
I. Bretton-Granatoor, Gary M.
BM534.J49 1997
296.3'9—DC21   96–47481
                                                                CIP

This book is printed on acid-free paper
Copyright © 1997 by the UAHC Press
Manufactured in the United States of America
10 9 8 7 6 5 4 3 2 1

Contents

Introduction   1

About the Program   4

Session 1
Introduction to the Issues   7
Video: *The Wave*

Session 2
The Characteristics of a Cult   14

Session 3
Comparing Cults to Mainstream Religions 19

Session 4
Jewish Ideals and Values That Challenge Cults 22

Session 5
Destructive Versus Nondestructive Cults 26

Session 6
Why Do People Join Cults? 41
Video: *Ticket to Heaven*

Session 7
Why Jews Join Cults   60
Video: *You Can Go Home Again*

Session 8
Who Recruits and Why?   64

Session 9
Techniques of Recruitment   70

Session 10
The Development of the Messianic Idea
and the Jewish Position on Jesus   78

Session 11
How to Respond to Christian Missionaries
and the Proof Texts They Use   86

Session 12
Concluding Activity
Include or Exclude Jews Involved in Cults from
Synagogue and Community Membership?   110

Appendix I   114

Appendix II   118
Cult-Awareness Organizations

A
JEWISH
RESPONSE TO
CULTS

❖

Introduction

If you remember the early 1970s, then you probably also remember it as the decade in which there was a growing concern among parents, rabbis, and Jewish educators about the increasing number of young people expressing interest in cults. What especially caught the attention of these adults was the sophisticated use by cults of pyramid power structures and their hypnotic effect on teenagers. For once teenagers had joined a cult, it was only a matter of time before they broke off all contact with their families and friends, refusing to leave. Scarier yet, even when they expressed an interest in leaving, these groups quickly erected mental and physical barriers that made leaving impossible.

To combat this growing problem, Rabbi Alexander M. Schindler appointed Annette Daum, z"l, as staff director to the Task Force on Cults and Missionaries, which was chaired by former UAHC board member Harry Helft. Working with rabbis in the field, parents, and lay people, Annette organized the UAHC's response to missionaries and cult recruiters targeting our children. She also traveled extensively around the country to speak to confirmation classes and youth groups, published educational materials, and worked with cult awareness organizations. Shortly before her untimely death, Annette had just finished work on *The*

Target Is You, the UAHC videotape on the missionary efforts of Hebrew-Christians.

For more than four years, I had the privilege of serving as Annette Daum's successor, leading the UAHC's Department of Interreligious Affairs. By the time I assumed the position, the conventional wisdom was that we had little to fear from cults and missionary groups. However, shortly after I began, it became clear that cults had not disappeared at all, they had merely changed their targets and techniques. Where before we had faced mostly religious cults, we now found ourselves dealing with a growing number of political and business-oriented cults. Teenagers, senior citizens, empty nesters, and young professionals were all targeted in this new wave of cult recruitment. The "love-bombing" of the '70s had evolved into the highly sophisticated advertising campaigns of the '80s and '90s. Soon we began to hear not just from the parents of teenagers and college students, but from spouses, business associates, and the children of aging parents. No longer could we ignore the fact that cults were expanding in new and unexpected directions.

When our communities' problem with cults first began, the solution as we saw it then was education. Education is still the solution and is needed more than ever. This text, based on the work done by Annette Daum two decades ago, was specifically created to provide teenagers with the means to respond to the empty promises of cult recruiters and missionaries. It is my hope that with the knowledge our children will gain from within these pages, they will develop healthy Jewish identities so no parent, child, spouse, or friend will ever have to face the terrible ordeal of rescuing a loved one from a cult or missionary group.

This book was the result of much hard work on the part of many individuals. Thanks are owed to Judith Goldman, Rabbi Barbara Metzinger, and Rabbi Ellen Nemhauser for their extensive editorial work. Thanks also go to Elise Kahn, who served as a research assistant on this project. Our most important debt, however, is to Rabbi Zari Weiss, who helped us find our way as we began work on this volume. We thank her for her time and effort in making this book possible.

Gary Bretton-Granatoor
Senior Rabbi, Stephen Wise Free Synagogue
New York City
Pesach 5756, Passover 1996

About the Program

The program, as outlined herein, is aimed primarily at high-school-aged teenagers but may be used with college-aged students and older members of the Jewish communities in which you live. In the next several weeks, participants in this program will explore the cult phenomenon, both in the United States and abroad. Students will examine a series of topics, including the following:

- What types of groups are generally considered cults and the differences between destructive and nondestructive cults.
- The differences between cults and other groups, including those defined as normative religions.
- The reasons why people are attracted to and join cults.
- The times when individuals are most vulnerable to the recruiting tactics of cults.
- The possible reasons why a disproportionate number of Jews are involved in cults or cult-like groups.
- The techniques and methods cults and cult-groups use to recruit new members, as well as the reasons why members participate in recruiting potential members.
- The potential benefits and risks (psychological, spiritual, social, financial) of cult involvement.

- The troubling question of religious fundamentalism and why religious fundamentalism in any denomination is cause for concern.
- The question of "Jews for Jesus," with a particular emphasis on the established Jewish position on Jesus and the phenomenon of Jews who accept Jesus today.
- The many miscellaneous cult or cult-like groups out there, including Jewish cult groups, occult/Satanic groups, and those associated with the New Age movement.

In preparing this program, facilitators should be prepared for anything. Much of the matter included is sure to touch a nerve in the more sensitive areas of a participant's life. At the same time, there are also sure to be many students—too many, in fact—who will be convinced that they are immune to the wiles of cults and cult-like groups. Do not let them be fooled. Anyone can become a cult member, even those who seem strongest among our friends or relatives. If there is anything this program is designed to teach, it is that we as human beings all have our weak moments, our points of vulnerability, and we must forever be on our guard to prevent recruiters associated with cults and cult-like groups from taking advantage of those all-too-human moments in our lives.

Introduction to the Issues

Goals
- To experience some of the inherent dangers of a cult-like group mentality.
- To stimulate students to explore some of the issues surrounding such group association and to understand how these issues affect people's personal lives.
- To make students aware of the risks they or their friends and loved ones face through involvement with cults.

Objectives

Students will be able to:
- Explain why some individuals identify with cult-like groups and some do not.
- Identify those moments when individuals are particularly vulnerable to the influence of cult-like groups.
- List those factors that make cult-like groups effective.
- Describe the "benefits" participants presumably derive from membership in a cult-like group.
- Describe the ways in which cults foster and develop a "group mentality."

- Describe the risks run by those who voice disagreement with the group or its teachings, as well as the risks posed to those who accept the group's teachings fully and unconditionally.
- Describe what effect learning the true nature of the group and its teachings can have upon individuals.

Materials
1. Video: *The Wave*, 46 mins. (See Appendix I.)
2. Handout: "Discussion Guide to *The Wave*" (pp. 10–13).

Activities
1. The following paragraph includes background information about cults that the teacher may want to share with students:

    It is estimated that there are approximately 3,000 cults in the United States today. While some of these groups are considered neither destructive nor harmful, some do involve their members in illegal or unethical practices, from mind control and manipulation to various forms of abuse and violence (including sexual abuse, child abuse, and forced prostitution). Cults or cult-like groups also often have their members participate in fraudulent and deceitful recruiting, business, financial, and fund-raising activities, as well as drug dealing and illegal immigration.

2. Show students the movie *The Wave*. (Approximate viewing time is 46 minutes. For further information, see Appendix I.) Students are likely to react strongly to this film, so it is important to highlight some specific points. The teacher should use the following question guide to facilitate discussion. Consider, for example, leading a debate in which groups of students each address a different question or group of questions.

3. Discussion wrap-up: *The Wave* is an excellent dramatization of what can happen when individuals become involved in cults or cult-like groups. The film shows:

- The ways in which a group mentality is fostered and developed;
- The factors that make a group attractive to followers;
- Why people are vulnerable to this type of group activity, as well as the ways in which peer pressure can influence even the most emotionally solid individuals to join a cult-like group;
- The characteristics of a group leader and why individuals are drawn to this type of leader;
- The supposed "benefits" of group membership;
- What can happen to those who question or disagree with the group's teachings or ways; and
- The harmful effects participation in such a group can have on its members.

DISCUSSION GUIDE TO *THE WAVE*

1. What was the name of the group in the film?
The Wave.

2. Who was the group's leader?
The social studies teacher.

3. Who were the initial members?
The students in his social studies class.

4. Why did the members (of the class) follow the leader (their teacher)?
He commanded authority and set clear, firm rules. His voice and body language conveyed power and confidence. He was already an "authority" figure. He capitalized on their personal strengths and weaknesses in sports and academics. He provided a structure and a way of behaving that appealed to many and filled a void for some.

5. Upon what philosophy/teaching was the group based?
"Strength through discipline, strength through community, strength through action."

6. What messages did these slogans convey?
Discipline was the key to power and success; the way to achieve power was to mobilize energy and resources by being active; conformity to the group was essential and dissension unacceptable. These presumably benefited the students by increasing their self-esteem as individuals and as a group.

7. How did the members of the group express these teachings?
By repeating the slogans; by changing their body language, their dress, and their behavior; and by adopting a military-like conformity.

8. How were these teachings reinforced?
Through repetition, the adoption of an authoritative and confident tone of voice, and personal "testimonies" to the benefits of the teachings to their lives.

9. What was the special sign that showed that one was a member of the group?
A hand signal.

10. **What was the symbol that the group used in its literature?**

A wave.

11. **What did this symbol represent?**

Movement and momentum; the "wave of the future"; "the wave is upon us."

12. **As more people began to accept the group, its teachings, and the leader's authority, how did the behavior of the leader change?**

He began to appreciate the power he had acquired; he became grandiose; he forgot the original purpose of his experiment.

13. **What effect did the group and its teachings have upon the members?**

Members grew more self-confident; they began to care more about how they dressed and carried themselves; they acquired a sense of "purpose."

14. **How did their body language change? How did their attitudes change? How did their self-images change?**

While they were in class, they stood tall and assumed a very "proper" gait. They also started to seek a greater conformity in their dress.

15. **What effect did the group have on the class "nerd"?**

The group made the class "nerd" feel as if he were a part of things, as if he were also important and valuable. Later, as a result, he, too, began to pay more attention to the way he looked and carried himself.

16. **Were these changes seen by the members as positive?**

Yes, as evidenced by the members' personal "testimonies" of the ways in which The Wave had affected their lives and their class.

17. **Why might others ("outsiders") have wanted to become members of the group?**

In order to feel as if they belonged and were a part of something "cool"; to reap the "benefits" of group membership.

18. **Were there any members of the class who maintained their individuality, who didn't accept the group's teachings or its required behavior?**

Initially, only Laurie; later, her boyfriend.

19. **What caused Laurie to question what was happening?**
The conversation with her parents.

20. **What values did Laurie's mother try to remind Laurie of?**
To think for herself; to question; to use her own mind and reasoning abilities to make decisions for herself.

21. **How did Laurie's father respond to Laurie's participation in The Wave?**
He thought the experiment harmless; he even thought it might have some positive effects upon the students in the long run.

22. **What happened to those who openly disagreed?**
They were ostracized, rejected, or "expelled."

23. **Did Laurie's resistance to the group's ways place her in jeopardy? Emotionally? Physically?**
Yes, her resistance jeopardized her relationships with her friends, her classmates, her boyfriend; it even jeopardized her physical safety.

24. **What happened when Laurie tried to reason with members of the group? How did they respond to her, and why did they respond that way?**
They felt threatened and tried to persuade her not to speak out against the group. They were afraid she might destroy something that had become important and meaningful to them.

25. **What were members of the group willing to do to "silence" Laurie?**
Scare her, threaten her physically.

26. **Why do you think Laurie's boyfriend was finally able to come to his senses?**
He finally realized that the group had made him do something he would not have otherwise done—physically hurt someone for whom he cared deeply.

27. **What was the teacher's reaction when Laurie and David came to talk to him?**

He was awakened from the power-mad state into which he had fallen.

28. **Do you think the teacher was fully aware of the effect the group was having on the students? Why do you think he did not end the experiment earlier?**

   Though he seemed to be aware of the experiment's effect on the group, he also appeared unable to remove himself from the experiment. And because he also wanted to see how far he could take the experiment, he needed to end it his own way.

29. **What lesson was the teacher trying to teach the members of the group by showing them the film on Hitler?**

   He tried to teach them that their willingness to accept the statements of an authority figure as "truths" or "lies" could ultimately lead to the type of madness perpetrated by Hitler. He also demonstrated to them how quickly they surrendered their individuality to the greater "cause," one that was ultimately destructive to themselves and others.

30. **What effect do you think the film on Hitler had on the students? How did they respond?**

   It devastated them, destroying the world of meaning they had created for themselves. They were left bereft as all in which they had invested—emotionally and physically—came crashing down on them, with nothing to fill its place.

31. **Who was the most devastated by the revelation? Why?**

   The class "nerd" appeared to be the most devastated, largely because the group had given him a sense of belonging and self-worth he had never had before.

32. **Do you think this experiment had any long-lasting effects upon those who had become members of the group? Explain why or why not. Was the teacher right or wrong to conduct such an experiment? Was this a responsible use of his authority?**

   These are open questions that students should seriously ponder.

The Characteristics of a Cult

Goals
- To introduce students to the characteristics of cults and cult-like groups.
- To explore which aspects of certain groups should be cause for concern.
- To provide students with a list of organizations identified with possessing cult-like tendencies.
- To explore the characteristics of some of these organizations.

Objectives
Students will be able to:
- List the characteristics of cults and cult-like groups.
- Identify these characteristics in cult-like organizations.
- Describe some of the characteristics of a leader of a cult-like group.

Materials
1. Information packets containing 40–60 pages of journal, magazine, and newspaper articles on cult groups, marked with anasterisk (*) in Activity 2. (See Appendix I.)
2. Handout: "Characteristics of Cults" (pp. 17–18).

Activities
1. Briefly review the last session and the class's discussion of The Wave.
2. Write on the chalkboard or a large piece of butcher paper the names of the groups listed below. (Please note that this list includes some groups that are not considered cults.)

Unification Church (Moonies)
Scientology°
The Children of God°
Hare Krishna°
Transcendental Meditation
Jews for Jesus
Campus Life
The Forum (formerly EST)°
Church Universal and Triumphant°
Messianic Judaism (Chosen People
   Ministries and Ariel
   Ministries)
Lubavitich Chasidism

LaRouche front groups°
Jehovah's Witness
Synanon
Divine Light Mission°
The Way International°
Hebrew-Christian groups
CampusAdvance/International
Churches of Christ
MOVE
Rajneesh Movement°
Branch Davidians (David Koresh)
Mormons

3. Draw up with students a separate list of aspects that might indicate cult-like activity. (Use the following list of questions to help students define those aspects.) Flag in some manner those groups the students think exhibit one or more of the aspects listed.
   - What is the leader of the group like (authoritarian, egocentric, male/female)?
   - Is the group led by one or more persons?
   - What is the decision-making process (democratic, authoritarian, etc.)?
   - Does the leader make claims about himself or herself?
   - Does the leader admit to making mistakes?
   - What does the leader ask of followers?
   - How do the members feel about the leader?

- How are new members obtained? How are existing members retained?
- What are the group's principal teachings? What is its way of life?
- What claims does the group make about itself?
- Do outsiders or ex-members charge the group with any wrongdoing? With illegal or unethical activities? How does the group's leadership respond to these charges?
- Have members of the group been arrested?

4. Hand out "Characteristics of Cults" (pp. 17–18). Be sure to indicate that not all cults have all of these characteristics. After all, there is no one definition of a cult. Cults can grow out of any set of ideas or beliefs. The ideas need not be unfamiliar or strange. Defining a cult is a question of how its members act or behave, not a question of what its members believe.[1] (The following list of cult characteristics was taken from a variety of sources.[2])

5. Read through the list and discuss.

1. See Marcia R. Rudin, *Too Good to Be True: Resisting Cults and Psychological Manipulation, A Lesson Plan for Middle Schools and High Schools* (New York: International Cult Education Program, 1992).

2. These sources include Rachel Andres and James R. Lane, eds., *Cults and Consequences: The Definitive Handbook* (Los Angeles: Commission on Cults and Missionaries of the Jewish Federation Council of Greater Los Angeles, 1988) and Sandy Andron, *Cultivating Cult-Evading* (Miami: Central Agency for Jewish Education, 1983).

CHARACTERISTICS OF CULTS

Cults are ...

- Often a group of people who follow a living leader, usually one who is male, dominant, and/or paternal. Occasionally leadership is shared by a pair or a "family" of leaders. Leaders often make absolute claims about their characters, abilities, and knowledge. Claims made by leaders may include any or all of the following:
  * that they are divine (i.e., God incarnate or the Messiah).
  * that they are the sole agents of the divine on earth and, therefore, God's agents or emissaries.
  * that they are omniscient and infallible and, thus, the possessors of absolute truth and total wisdom.
- Groups in which members develop a deep emotional dependence upon the group or its leader.
- Groups in which the response of the leader or leaders to members of the group is often erratic, making the members unsure of their standing in the group.
- Often deceptive in their recruiting practices.

Cults often may...

- Employ various techniques of thought reform or mind control.
- Exploit members' skills, abilities, and talents.
- Allow mingling with outsiders only for recruiting and fund-raising purposes.
- Engender fear, hatred, and suspicion of nonmembers (including the families and friends of members).
- Demand a firm commitment to join before the recruit has a chance to think it over carefully or consult with family, friends, or other trusted advisers.
- Attempt to discredit and denounce other religions.
- Claim a vision that is millennial or apocalyptic. (The fixation on the coming of the millennium refers to the thousand years mentioned in the New Testament Book of Revelation, chapter 20, during which holiness is to prevail and Jesus is to reign on earth.

An apocalyptic vision is prophetic and forecasts the ultimate destiny of the world.)

- Maintain their membership through psychological coercion by refusing to respect an individual's autonomy.
- Deprive their followers of normal health-sustaining practices (often by altering their diet and rest patterns).
- Respond to critics with intimidation and/or physical or legal threats.

Comparing Cults to Mainstream Religions

Goals
- To understand the basic structures and principles of the mainstream religions in America.
- To distinguish cults from mainstream religions.

Objectives
Students will be able to:
- Describe the basic structures and principles of the major religions in America.
- State those characteristics not found in most normative religions.
- Compare and contrast cults and mainstream religions.

Materials
Handout: "Most Normative Religions Don't ..." (p. 21).

Activities
1. Briefly review the last session with the students. If it has not yet been completed, have the students finish filling in the butcher paper chart comparing the characteristics of the various groups, some of which are considered by experts in the field to be cults.

2. Divide students into groups to study the major religions in America (Catholicism, Protestantism, Judaism, Islam, and Buddhism) using articles from *World Religions in America*. (See Appendix I.) Students should be prepared to comment on the following, based on their research:
   - Leaders within the religions
   - Rituals
   - The role of conformity
   - Language/vocabulary
   - Dogma and the ability of adherents to question tenets (and their authority)
   - Membership (elitism)
3. Discuss the following questions:
   - *Why are some groups labeled cults?*
   Many groups have characteristics that appear to be cult-like. For example, most have leaders who inspire confidence and trust in their followers. The difference, therefore, is one of degree.[1]
   - *Is it possible that religions now popularly regarded as established or respectable might once, in their early history, have been considered cults? Why are they not seen as cults today?*
   Judaism, Christianity, and Islam have formalized religious doctrines and holy scriptures that may not be altered or arbitrarily rewritten by any one religious leader, regardless of his or her rank. (For example, the Lubavitcher Rebbe could not, by himself, change *halachah* so he could move Shabbat to Wednesday.)
4. Hand out the list "Most Normative Religions Don't …" (p. 21). Have students take turns reading each item aloud and giving a tangible example for each item. (Their example should come from their research on the various groups.)
5. Summarize on the board. Ask the students if they think cults are different from normative religions (Christianity, Judaism, Islam, Buddhism, etc.), and if so, how?

1. See Sandy Andron, *Cultivating Cult-Evading*, p. 10.

MOST NORMATIVE RELIGIONS DON'T ...

- Equate doubt with guilt.
- Substitute an infallible person for an ethical document of faith.
- Deprive one of one's personal belongings, privacy, or personal space.
- Practice honesty within and trickery without.
- Fear and reject questioning, critical thinking, and analysis.
- Suggest that fulfillment or transcendence comes from thought elimination.
- Call for personality change and puppet-like conformity.
- Call for blind and unquestioning obedience.
- Deprive members of adequate nutrition, sleep, or health care.
- Claim to have solutions to all of life's cares and problems.
- Work exclusively for the financial benefit of a single individual or leader.
- Offer simple answers to complex problems.
- Have extraordinarily narrow definitions or rules for following the religion. (Indeed, most normative religions often contain variations or strains within themselves.)

Jewish Ideals and Values
That Challenge Cults

Goals
- To explore Jewish ideals and values as exemplified in the Ten Commandments and other biblical verses.
- To use these ideals and values to challenge cult-like group behavior.

Objectives
Students will be able to:
- List the Ten Commandments.
- Explain the meaning of certain biblical verses and how they apply to our lives today.
- Identify Jewish ideals and values that challenge cult-like group behavior, such as showing respect for one's parents, allowing others the freedom to choose, not bearing false witness, recognizing the spiritual and physical freedom of individuals.

Materials
A *Tanach* for each group to use during Activities 2 and 3.

Activities
1. Briefly review the last session. Ask students what are some of the ways in which "mainstream" religions differ from cults?

2. Have students do the two following linked activities:

   a. Dramatization: Divide the students into pairs and have each pair act out one of the following scenarios:
  - Noah/God's voice (Genesis 6:13–7:17)
  - Abraham/God's voice (regarding the destruction of Sodom and Gomorrah, Genesis 18:16–33)
  - Moses/God's voice (regarding God's call to Moses to go to Pharaoh, Exodus 3:1–14)
  - Job/God's voice (Job 1:13–22; 2:7–10; 2:11–3:26; 38:1–42:6)
  - Jonah/God's voice (Jonah 1:1–3; 2:2–3:3; 3:10–4:11)

   b. Discuss the three questions below in the context of the dramatized passages and these two key biblical passages:

"Surely, if you do right, there is uplift. But if you do not do right, sin couches as the door; its urge is toward you, yet you can be its master." (Genesis 4:7)

"I call heaven and earth to witness against you this day: I have put before you life and death, blessing and curse. Choose life—if you and your offspring would live." (Deuteronomy 30:19)

  - What does Jewish tradition seem to say about questioning?
  - What does Jewish tradition say about individual responsibility and free choice?
  - How does this attitude differ from what we've learned about cult-like groups in which dissension is not allowed?

3. Use the following exercises to have students review and discuss basic biblical commandments and values.[1]

   a. Ask students to explain the meaning of "You shall not bear

---

1. Taken from the UAHC Department of Interreligious Affairs, *Missionary and Cult Movements: A Mini-Course for Upper Grades in Religious Schools* (New York: UAHC, 1982).

false witness against your neighbor." (Exodus 20:13) Ask them if they think there is some wisdom or value to this rule. Why or Why not? Give examples of this in your own life.

b. Have students explain the meaning of the biblical verse: "You shall not side with the majority to do wrong." (Exodus 23:2) Ask them if they think there is some wisdom or value to this rule. In recent years, what are some ways in which people have sided with the majority to do wrong? (Push them beyond the example of the Holocaust.) The traditional understanding of this verse is offered by Rashi, who asserts "Do not follow a majority blindly if your conscience demands otherwise." Ask the students how some might blindly follow a majority or put unquestioned trust in a majority today.

c. Challenge the students to list the Ten Commandments. (Exodus 20:1–14) Ask them which of the Ten Commandments are ignored when one becomes a member of a cult. Which Jewish ideals and values challenge cult-group behaviors? Use the following examples:

- Obedience to God alone: "You shall have no other gods besides Me. You shall not make for yourself a sculptured image, or any likeness of what is in the heavens above, or on the earth below, or in the waters under the earth. You shall not bow down to them or serve them." (Exodus 20:3–5)
- Questioning authority: our biblical heroes—Noah, Abraham, Moses, Job, Jonah—even questioned God.
- Individual responsibility and free choice: Genesis 4:7 and Deuteronomy 30:19.
- Not bearing false witness: Exodus 20:13.

2. W. Gunther Plaut, ed., *The Torah: A Modern Commentary* (New York: UAHC Press, 1981), p. 580, n. 2.

- Not exerting peer pressure: Exodus 23:2.
- Respect for parents and family: "Honor your father and your mother" (Exodus 20:12); "You shall each revere his mother and his father" (Leviticus 19:3); and "He [Elijah] shall reconcile fathers with sons and sons with their fathers." (Malachi 3:24)
- Commitment to physical and spiritual freedom: "I am the Lord your God who brought you out of the land of Egypt, the house of bondage." (Exodus 20:2)

SESSION **5**

Destructive Versus Nondestructive Cults

Goals
- To distinguish between destructive and nondestructive cults.
- To identify those characteristics that make a cult harmful.
- To become familiar with various types of cults.

Objectives
Students will be able to:
- Compare and contrast characteristics of the groups to which they belong with those of destructive cults.
- List those characteristics that make a cult harmful.
- Name and define the various categories of destructive cults.
- Name five well-known destructive cults.

Materials
Handout: Essay by Corey Slavin (pp. 34-40).

Activities
1. Briefly review the list of Jewish values and ideals compiled in the last session.
2. Read the article by Corey Slavin aloud in class. Have the students take turns reading aloud or ask someone to play the part of Corey. It might be helpful to arrange the latter with the

student several days before the class so that he or she might develop the role better. Alternatively, stage the article as a play or interview. Or set up a "talk show" in which Corey and/or cult members are interviewed by a talk show host.

3. Discuss the following questions:
   - How did Corey become distanced from her family and friends?
   - Did this happen overnight?
   - Do you think she was aware of what was happening as it was happening?
   - From what you've learned, how do the practices of many cults—including the one to which Corey belonged—contradict Judaism's dictum to honor one's parents?
   - Among your friends and/or classmates, do you think there is anyone who might be identified as a "Corey"? Why or why not?

4. We all belong to groups of various kinds. Have students list across the top of a piece of paper the groups with which they are affiliated. Then they should add to this row the heading "Corey's Experience."

   Though the groups listed by the class are unlikely to be dangerous or harmful, how can students know for sure? There are criteria by which we can measure the potential danger of a group. As the following questions are read, the students should write their answers under the groups they have listed on their paper. (For the column "Corey's Experience," reread the questions, replacing "you" with "Corey.")

   - Were you told the real name of the group when you joined it?
   - Were you told outright who was the leader (president, chairperson, etc.)?
   - Was there anything about the group that was hidden from you when you joined it?
   - Were you forced to join?

- Were you free to make your own decisions or choices?
- Was there a way for you or anyone else to voice an opinion or criticism?
- Were you told to reject your family or your family's values?
- What happens if the behavior of the group's leader gets out of control? What can be done?
- Did any of these questions make you think twice about any of the groups to which you belong? (Note: This is a serious question that may reveal important information about the students' affiliations with questionable groups. Cults seek out high school students, as well as college students and the elderly.)
- How did Corey's experience fare in light of these questions? If you were Corey and had known to ask these questions beforehand, do you think you would have known that the group she had joined was a dangerous cult?

5. Drawing on the previous lessons and exercises, have the students create a list of characteristics that would indicate a specific group is potentially harmful. Use the following list as a guide.

   a. Deception
      - Cults commonly recruit new members and engage in fund-raising activities without fully disclosing the use of mind-controlling techniques or the real nature of the organization.
      - They often hide behind various front groups.
      - They are frequently secretive or vague with regard to the true nature of their beliefs and activities.
      - They generally lie in order to get members to join and stay.

   b. Mind Control
      - They attack an individual's ability to think independently through coercion, behavior-modification techniques, or persuasive pressure.

- They practice these techniques without the informed consent of the individual.

  c. Exclusivity

    - They isolate the individual.
    - They demand through subtle and not-so-subtle means that the individual separate physically and emotionally from family, friends, and society and that this person substitute the group as a new family.
    - They insist that the individual replace his or her previous values and beliefs with those of the group.

  d. Exploitation and Abuse

    - They take advantage of the individual's vulnerability by exploiting that person financially, physically, emotionally, or sexually.
    - They deprive new recruits or members of adequate food, sleep, and time to think in order to break their spirits and win their allegiance.

  e. Allegiance

    - They demand complete obedience and dependence on the group or its leader(s).
    - They place the welfare and well-being of the group before that of the individual.
    - They claim that all activities—including those that are unethical or illegal—are acceptable and necessary because they are for the good of the group or the leader.
    - They use guilt and threats as punishment for disobedience

6. Harmful or destructive cults are both religious and nonreligious in nature. Destructive cults fall into several categories:

  a. Religious

    - Religious cults are generally the best known and most numerous.[1] They focus on religious dogma, basing their beliefs either on the Bible, Eastern religions, or the oc-

---

1. This section was compiled from Steven Hassan, *Combatting Cult Mind Control* (Rochester, VT: Park Street Press, 1988), pp. 39–40 and Michael D. Langone, ed., *Recovery from Cults* (New York and London: W. W. Norton & Co., 1993), p. 254.

cult. They are often "contemporary versions of the ancient Christian heresy known as Gnosticism, the teaching that one can only be saved by special enlightenment, the privilege of the spiritually elite." But despite an emphasis on spirituality, these cults just as often focus on the material world, as evidenced by the luxurious life-styles of their leaders and their ownership and control of millions of dollars of real estate and business assets. "Most religious cults deny the claims of Judaism to be the fullness of God's revelation. Each of these cults has a leader who claims to complete the job of saving humanity and to provide the fullness of revealed truth. Therefore, from their point of view, the Holy Bible is inadequate, just as mainstream synagogues and churches are inadequate as fellowships to nurture souls to salvation." Examples of religious cults include the Unification Church, the Church of Scientology, Church Universal and Triumphant, The Way International, and Rajneesh.

b. Psychotherapy/Educational
- Therapy cults have leaders who claim they can help people solve their personal problems and fulfill their followers' potential; they sometimes give medical advice, practice medicine, or use hypnosis. "Psychotherapy/educational cults hold workshops and seminars for hundreds of dollars to provide 'insight' and 'enlightenment.' They use many basic mind control techniques to provide participants with a 'peak experience.'" Graduates are then encouraged to enroll in more expensive advanced courses that serve to enmesh them in the group. Once committed to the group, members are then told to recruit their friends, relatives, and co-workers or to cut off relationships with them.[2] Recruiters, however, are not allowed to

2. *Combatting Cult Mind Control*, p. 40.

disclose much about the program. Examples of this type of cult include The Forum and Lifespring.

c. Political
  - Political cults "are organized around a particular political dogma" or ideology. "They often make the news, usually with the word 'fringe' or 'extremist' attached," and are distinguished by their "deceptive recruitment and mind control practices."[3] Frequently they are involved in building up arsenals of weapons, teaching survivalist techniques, and supporting the overthrow of the United States government. Examples of political cults include Lyndon LaRouche groups, MOVE, Aryan Nation, the Michigan Militia, and other paramilitary groups.

d. Commercial
  - Commercial cults deceive and manipulate individuals into working for little or no pay in the hope of getting rich. These cults can include pyramid-style or multilevel marketing organizations whose "success depends on recruiting new people who in turn recruit others. Other commercial cults include those that browbeat people into hawking magazines and other items door to door."[4] These cults promise exciting travel and lucrative careers. Then, through fear, guilt, and sometimes physical and sexual abuse, they manipulate salespeople into becoming slaves to the "company" and turning over all of their earnings and savings in order to pay "living expenses."

e. New Age
  - New Age cults include most psychotherapy cults. They exploit members' "personal anxieties that have been made more painful and persistent by a strained social environment.... The essence of the New Age vision that captivates these seekers is that meaning ... is primarily an emotional experience; it is not necessary to be logical,

3. Ibid., p. 40.
4. Ibid., p. 40.

rational, or even reasonable. [Thus] what is good is a to-tally subjective feeling-state. The goal of life becomes a good feeling, a never-ending 'high.'" New Age recruits are frequently blind to the sophisticated psychological tech-niques cult leaders use to manipulate that feeling. These techniques include channeling ("presumably a psychic form of communication with the dead or disembodied spirits") and various types of hypnosis.[5]

f. Satanism and Ritual Abuse

Satanism currently covers a broad range of activities, includ-ing the following:

- Formal or informal worship of Satan or entities equated with or associated with Satan and/or violence, cruelty, and destructiveness.

- The practice of black magic (the manipulation of alleged magical forces for destructive ends).

- Preoccupation with literature, symbols, rituals, or other artifacts and activities associated with Satan or related entities, or with black magic.

- Attempts to enhance sexual, criminal, or other activities by participation in rituals associated with the worship of Satan or related entities, or with the practice of black magic.

- Ritualistic abuse, such as the sexual abuse of children, "that occurs in a context linked to certain symbols or group activity that has a religious, magical, or supernatural connotation, and where the invocation of these symbols or activities is repeated over time and used to frighten and intimidate children."[6]

- Examples of Satanic cults include The Church of Satan, Abraxas Foundation, and The Temple of Set.

5. Ibid., p. 195 and *Recovery from Cults*, pp. 182–188.

6. From Michael D. Langone and Linda O. Blood, *Satanism and Occult-Related Violence: What You Should Know* (Weston, MA: American Family Foundation, 1990), p. 81.

7. Optional Homework: Over the next week (or possibly during the remainder of their study of cults), ask students to look for articles in newspapers and magazines on cults. Students should photocopy, if possible, the article and be prepared to give a brief summary of it to the rest of the class.

HOW DID A NICE JEWISH GIRL
GET RECRUITED INTO A CULT?

Corey Slavin

Not long ago I was at a dinner party and at the other end of the table I could hear a guy mention the word "cult" (or as my mother lovingly refers to it—the "C" word). I stopped talking and began eavesdropping on a conversation about the "freaks" who get involved in cults.

A friend touched my arm. "Don't say something you'll regret," she whispered.

"I think what you meant to say is don't say something he'll regret," I said as I pointed to the guy at the other end of the table. I then turned away from my friend and said, "Excuse me, but I was in a cult, and I would hardly describe myself as a freak. Not then and not now."

• • •

People often think that people who get recruited into cults are drug addicts, hippies, homeless, or people on the fringes of society. But that's not true, as I am the epitome of the perfect cult recruit. I was deceptively recruited into Church Universal and Triumphant (CUT), a paramilitaristic religious cult that combines New Age religion, Buddhism, Christianity, and Catholicism. The leader of the cult is Elizabeth Clare Prophet—the self-proclaimed Queen of the New Age Movement.

And me? What was I like when I got recruited into a cult? I was a nice Jewish girl.

• • •

I grew up in Los Angeles, in the San Fernando Valley, and have a younger brother. My family belonged to a Reform congregation where I attended religious school, became a bat mitzvah, was confirmed, graduated from high school, and later taught religious school. I also went to a Jewish summer camp for 12 years, as a camper and a counselor.

Judaism was very important to me, and often when people asked me if I would call myself an American or a Jew first, my response was "Jew."

I received my bachelor of arts in history from the University of California at San Diego in 1985. My specialty was Chinese history. Then I moved back to Los Angeles, where I started working in public relations. I lived with a friend for a couple of years until 1988, when I decided I wanted to live by myself. I rented an apartment about a mile away from my parents. At the same time I got a job as Director of Public Relations for Hy's Century City—an expensive steak house.

In April 1988, my grandmother died. She and I had been very close. I could tell her anything, and I admired and looked up to her. Her death made me question Judaism for the first time. I would ask myself, "Why are we here?" or "Why are Jews the chosen people?"—questions that I think most of us ask at one time or another. I didn't feel comfortable talking to my parents or brother about my feelings. And I didn't talk to my friends because they viewed me as a strong person, someone to whom they could come when they had problems. I was afraid that if I showed them how vulnerable I was, they wouldn't trust me anymore. So I started reading self-help books and books about Judaism.

At the restaurant where I worked I met Tamara, one of the restaurant's managers. Though she was only a year older than I was, the thing that stood out most about Tamara was how together her life was. She always knew what to say and what to wear. Nothing ever bothered her. At a time when I had no self-esteem, she wanted to be my friend.

Tamara and I became fast and inseparable friends. I stopped talking to and seeing my other friends. I started screening my calls and wouldn't talk to my family. Within a few weeks, all I had in my life was work and Tamara. She and I spent hours talking about everything—boyfriends, religion, music, movies, politics. At first she was very accepting of everything I felt and believed.

I told her that I was seeing a therapist, and she said, "I don't believe in therapy, but it seems to be helping you. Maybe I was wrong."

A few weeks later, out of the blue, she said to me, "Corey, you know more than your therapist. I don't know why you waste your money."

The next week I told my therapist that I was not going to continue with therapy anymore.

Tamara never told me that she was affiliated with any religion or church, but she would talk about all of these people in Montana who were just like me. She called them "lightbearers" or "chelas," which meant "followers of the path." She asked me how I felt about a female spiritual leader and did I think that the world could end.

"Anything is possible," I said.

"As a lightbearer you're obligated to save yourself," she said.

It turned out that saving myself meant I had to purchase a space in a fallout shelter for $6,500. The money came from an inheritance, and my father had to cosign on the account so I could get the money. I had to pay cash or with a cashier's check. I never got a receipt.

In August 1989, the decision was made that I was to move to Montana. I never felt as though I consciously made the decision myself. Tamara only gave me enough information to take the next step along the path she had created for me. Anytime I asked any questions, she made me feel stupid for doubting her. Besides, she was my best friend, how could I not trust my best friend to know what was right for me?

• • •

In January 1990, I quit my job, gave up my lease to the apartment, sold all my belongings, and literally picked up and moved to Montana without telling anyone. I called my parents from Las Vegas to tell them that I was on my way to my new home and that I was going to live with Tamara's family.

Once I got to Montana, I officially joined the Church Universal and Triumphant (CUT). I no longer had any control over my life. I was told what to wear, when to sleep, what to read, what movies to watch, and which music to listen to. I no longer watched TV. I was only allowed to eat rice and beans with some vegetables and a little fruit. Sugar, tobacco, and alcohol were forbidden, and I didn't eat any fish, meat, or poultry. Many times my personal letters were opened and read to me, and when I called home to talk to my parents, people would hover around me to listen in on my conversation.

I attended services where I learned to decree (a type of self-hypnotic fast-paced chanting) about four hours a day. The only books I read were by Elizabeth Clare Prophet.

On a typical day for me I would get up at 5:30 A.M., get dressed, have breakfast, and decree for two hours. Then I would go to help complete the fallout shelter (a lot of heavy manual labor). I'd have lunch around noon and work more on the shelter. At 3:00 P.M. every afternoon, I would go pick up Tamara's younger sister from school. She attended a school run by the cult. Then I would tutor her, have dinner, read, shower, decree for two more hours, and go to sleep at around midnight.

• • •

At first I was happy in Montana with my new friends, new family, and new religion. Life was exciting and different; each day a new experience. As time wore on, however, I began to miss my family and friends. I began to wish I were back in LA and that I could go to a movie or the theater. I longed to read a novel or watch anything on TV. I missed music. I wanted my old life back. But I could never tell anyone how I felt and I decreed whenever any of those feelings would pop up in my head. Doubts were unacceptable, and I believed that Elizabeth Clare Prophet could tell what I was thinking no matter where I was. I didn't want to disappoint her. I wanted to be the best "chela" in CUT.

On March 2, 1990, while lowering a table from the roof into the shelter, I had an accident. I fell and suffered a compound fracture to my wrist, a concussion, and a fractured hip. Although CUT doesn't believe in proper medical attention, I was taken to a nearby hospital where I wasn't treated properly. When the cast was taken off my wrist, my bone was protruding through my wrist.

I was told by CUT members that I had the accident because I wasn't holy enough but that I didn't die because I was in CUT. Then they told me that I didn't heal because I wasn't holy enough. The solution? To decree more. So I began to decree another two hours a day.

The period I was in Montana was called the "Prophecy Period." There were many days cited on which the world was going to end: March 15 and April 9, to name two. Obviously those days came and went and nothing happened.

On the first night—March 15—we were told to be in our assigned shelters by midnight. I saw a lot of people bring guns, semiautomatic rifles, and ammunition into the shelters. We were not told that the night in the shelter was just a drill. So I feared that this was it; the world would end and I would never see my parents again. I was scared.

Another time when the date passed and the world didn't end, we were told that all of our decrees to save the world had worked. But we were all decreeing for the world to end. Not one person questioned anything Elizabeth Clare Prophet told us.

Eventually in the middle of May we were told that if we didn't have jobs, we could return to our hometown, earn money, and then move back to Montana. Of course, I didn't have any money left. By the time I left Montana, I had given CUT more than $15,000.

I arrived unannounced at my parent's doorstep on May 18. My mother was so glad to see me she couldn't stop kissing and hugging me. She told me how skinny I looked. I guess I had lost a lot of weight, but I felt great. My brother immediately noticed that something was wrong with my wrist. So my parents sent me to three specialists, and I had to have bone replacement surgery.

Before the surgery I lived with my parents because I had nowhere else to go. But I spent most of my time with Tamara. There were moments I felt as though I was having a nervous breakdown. I knew there was something wrong with my life, but I just couldn't figure out what it was.

My parents seemed to be treating me differently as well. They were nicer. They appeared interested in my new religion and no longer called it a cult. My mother bought me clothes and my father offered me a job at his accounting firm.

I didn't know that they had gotten help through various Jewish organizations in Los Angeles. They even got involved in a support group for families with loved ones in cults.

• • •

One week after my surgery my mother took me to the doctor to have my cast put on and the stitches taken out of my arm and hip. When we got home from the doctor's office, I was surprised by two bodyguards who made me get back into my mother's car. I was taken to a "safe house" in Palm Springs where two deprogrammers met me. My brother and father were also there. I spent a weekend in Palm Springs sleeping when I wanted to and eating whatever I desired, whenever I wanted.

There was a part of me that was very relieved to be going through this debriefing. I was told many things about the cult that I never was told prior to joining, like the fact that the CUT is anti-Semitic. I read articles from newspapers and magazines about the cult and watched videotapes. I also learned about CUT's and Elizabeth Clare Prophet's illegal dealings.

Obviously if I had known any of this up front, I never would have gotten involved

• • •

I then spent a week in a rehabilitation center for former cult members where I had intensive therapy sessions during which I discussed my feelings of guilt, anger, depression and learned how to reacclimate to society.

Eventually I moved back in with my parents and lived with them for a year. I started therapy and joined a support group for former cult members. My family also went through family counseling. I was fortunate to get a job in public relations.

I spent a lot of time studying individually with rabbis so that I could relearn all the aspects of Judaism that had been distorted by my time in a religious cult.

• • •

More than five years later, I still celebrate the anniversary (August 2) of my leaving the cult. The date is more important than my birthday, because it was on that day that I got a new lease on life. I'm now friends with all of my old friends.

I've dedicated a lot of time to educating people about the dangers destructive cults pose. After all, if I could get recruited into a cult, anybody could.

In a lot of ways I am a much better person than I was before, and many of the scars have healed. Sometimes I wonder if I will ever again trust people wholeheartedly. Or if there will ever be a time when I won't look over my shoulder and wonder if someone is watching me. And I wonder if I'll ever date someone who doesn't initially cringe when I tell that person that I've been in a cult.

I appreciate everything I have—family, friends, possessions—and my religion more than I ever did. Every morning I count my blessings and think about the millions of people still trapped in cults.

Why Do People Join Cults?

Goals

- To examine our assumptions about people who join cults and about ourselves.
- To learn firsthand why someone joins a cult.
- To explore through the film *Ticket to Heaven* the process and techniques cults use to get people to join and stay involved.
- To understand that there are times in our lives when we are particularly vulnerable, and thus more susceptible, to the manipulative practices of cults.
- To explore this vulnerability and investigate possible responses to it.
- To understand that we always have choices.

Objectives

Students will be able to:

- Articulate their assumptions about those who join cults (and about themselves) at this point in their lives.
- Ask a former cult member why that person joined a cult and about his or her experiences in that cult.
- Describe the process and techniques (as illustrated in *Ticket to Heaven*) cults use to get people to join them.

- List points of vulnerability, such as the various transition times in our lives.
- List the people to whom we can turn when we feel vulnerable.

Materials
1. Questionnaire: "Some Questions to Think About" (pp. 45–46).
2. Handout: "How People Become Members of Cults" (pp. 47–48).
3. Handout: "Recruiting Techniques Used by Cults" (p. 49).
4. Video: *Ticket to Heaven*, 107 mins. (See Appendix I.)
5. Handout: "Discussion Guide to *Ticket to Heaven*" (pp. 50–59).

Activities
1. Ask the students if any of them has an article to share about a destructive cult (see Optional Homework in Session 5, p. 33). Spend approximately 5 to 10 minutes discussing articles and current events related to cults.
2. Because there are times in our lives when we are more susceptible to the manipulative practices of cults, ask students the following: From Corey Slavin's essay and other things they've read and learned, what might they consider vulnerable points in a person's life? Use the following list as a guide. (Please note that this session may be emotionally difficult for some students, depending upon events in their lives, their parents' lives, and their friends' lives. The teacher may, therefore, want to structure the discussion of the questions in small groups or as a writing exercise in which the student may speak more freely.)
   a. *Times of transition.* (These can include leaving for college for the first time; the death of a family member or a friend; divorce; the end of a significant relationship; the loss or change of a job; relocation to a new home; a bout with a serious illness.)
      - Are these points of vulnerability unusual?

- Do you expect to experience such points of vulnerability in your own life?
- Do you know anyone who is experiencing any of these points of vulnerability now?
- If someone you know is experiencing a vulnerable period right now, what can you do to help this person through it?

b. *Times when one is particularly lonely or depressed.*
- Have you ever experienced such a time in your life?
- How did you handle it?
- Was there someone with whom you could talk, someone who you felt really understood why you were lonely or depressed?
- What might someone who does not have a close or supportive family or group of friends do?

c. *Cult experts point out these additional vulnerable points.* Cults often appeal to people who are searching for meaning and purpose in life or hoping for a transcendent experience; are idealistic and want to improve the world; are frightened of the uncertainty of life today and of facing a difficult economy; want absolute, instant answers to life's complicated problems and ultimate questions; are attracted by a sense of daring and adventure; and are disillusioned with our political system and want to find another way to change the world.
- Do any of these descriptions apply to you? To someone you know?
- Do you think you are not susceptible to being drawn into a cult? Why or why not?

3. The purpose of the next exercise is to challenge assumptions we have about people who join cults. Hand out the questionnaire "Some Questions to Think About" (pp. 45–46) and give the students a few minutes to complete it privately. Afterwards, the students can decide whether they want to share their answers or not. Use the questionnaire either to stimulate

discussion or to elicit some hard thinking by the students on this subject.

4. Divide the students into small groups and hand out "How People Become Members of Cults" (pp. 47–48). Students should discuss the following questions:
   - Do you think you could ever be the victim of this type of mind control? Why or why not?
   - Do you think there is any value to this type of "spiritual discipline"? (Emphasize the extreme nature of the forms this discipline takes.)
   - Why do you think cults require this type of activity?

5. Bring the students back together and create a list of possible techniques a group might use to get a potential recruit to join it. Use "Recruiting Techniques Used by Cults" (p. 49) as a guide. (Once the teacher and students have generated the list, hand out the list for the students to keep.)

6. View video *Ticket to Heaven*.

7. Lead a discussion with the students using the "Discussion Guide to *Ticket to Heaven*" (pp. 50–59).

8. Optional Homework: Write a letter in response to a friend or sibling who has just gone off to college. This person has written you several letters about how lost, lonely, and depressed he or she is feeling in this new setting. It is the first time this person is away from family and friends. In your letter, give some advice—in an either direct or indirect way—about how to avoid getting drawn into a cult.

SOME QUESTIONS TO THINK ABOUT

1. People who join cults are weak and ignorant. (T/F)
2. At this point in my life, I think I have a strong sense of who I am and what I believe. (T/F)
3. I am unequivocally (that is, without doubt or hesitation) committed to Jewish tradition. (T/F)
4. I believe that everyone has a right to believe in what he or she wants to believe. (T/F)
5. I believe that everyone has a right to do what he or she wants to do. (T/F)
6. People who join cults are searching for something, such as meaning, a feeling of belonging, spiritual fulfillment, a substitute family, etc. (T/F)
7. I am strong willed and can resist anything. (T/F)
8. Only losers join cults. (T/F)
9. I would never feel so vulnerable that I would fall victim to the deceptive practices of a cult. (T/F)
10. I am easily influenced by others. (T/F)
11. Sometimes I can't make a decision and wish someone would make it for me. (T/F)
12. I do not easily succumb to peer pressure. (T/F)
13. When I go away to college, if I am asked by another college student, I could easily explain my Jewish beliefs (about sin, the Messiah, etc.). (T/F)
14. If someone invited me to a retreat about which I knew very little except that the people were very nice and that there would be cute guys or girls there, I would:
    a. go and check it out for myself.
    b. not go.
    c. find out about the group first.
15. When approached on the street or at my door by someone asking for money for an organization, I:
    a. always give when asked to donate money.

b. ask the nature of the organization before giving.

c. request to see some literature first.

16. If my parents told me they didn't want me to hang out with a group of people, I would:

a. honor their wishes and end my association.

b. continue to hang out with them, but in secret.

c. continue to hang out with them in open defiance of my parents.

17. When I feel vulnerable I ...

——.

18. One thing about Judaism that I do not like or find meaningful is ...

——.

19. If someone I knew joined a cult, I would ...

——.

HOW PEOPLE BECOME MEMBERS OF CULTS

Experts and former cult members say that people do not join cults just because they are unhappy or are searching for something. Those may be factors, but more important than these are the manipulative, pressuring, and deceptive tactics cults use to recruit people. These tactics are often examples of what we call "mind control" or "brainwashing."

How is it done? Most groups actively seek out new members by using slick sales pitches that employ glowing images of easy pathways to ecstasy and personal encounters with God, Jesus, or the group's own living "messiah." Once an individual is drawn into a cult, there is usually a single moment, rather than a process, of conversion. Conversion is almost always an intense experience that has been engineered through the skillful manipulation of information. A vivid example is the Hare Krishna's arti ka ceremony, in which new recruits, led by older members, perform a feverish jumping dance amid flickering lights, heavy incense, loud, droning music, and pounding drums until they are physically and emotionally overcome.

Next, most cults step up the indoctrination process, inculcating the group's beliefs and values at a time when the new convert is highly receptive. More important, at this stage, group leaders begin to implant those suggestions that are at the heart of the mind-control process. Calls to "surrender," "turn off the Satanic mind," or "let things float" act as covert hypnotic suggestions. If heeded, they can place the new convert in a continuous trance.

These simple self-hypnotic rituals close off the recruit's mind to doubts, questions, and disquieting memories of family and the outside world. They also produce a kind of ecstasy by default—a numbed, mindless high that many interpret as the attainment of their ultimate spiritual goal. But the price of this bliss may be incalculably high. It is here that the cult experience departs from what has always been respected as a valid religious or spiritual experience.

The most pronounced and startling effects of mind control are the bizarre disturbances it causes in a person's awareness, perception, memory, and other basic information-processing abilities. Former cult members complain of disorientation and "floating" in and out of altered states; recurrent nightmares, hallucinations, and delusions; bewildering and unnerving "psychic" phenomena; and an inability to break the mental rhythms, first introduced by the cult, of chanting, meditation, or speaking in tongues.

Without exception, the most compelling acts of cult life are the daily ritual or "therapeutic" practices required by every group. These methods vary widely according to cult: meditation in the Divine Light Mission; the act of "centering" on the teachings of Reverend Moon by Moonies; the "tongues" ritual in The Way; "training regiments" and "pastoral counseling" in Scientology; and the chanting of their familiar mantra by the Hare Krishnas. Respondents report spending from three to seven hours per day practicing one or more of these techniques. Members also report spending time each day in group rituals, including sensitivity sessions, psychodramas, guided fantasies, and a variety of emotion-filled confessional activities. Moreover, nearly all respondents report spending an additional 20 to 30 hours per week at lectures, seminars, workshops, or required private study sessions of cult doctrines. This grueling schedule of devotional activities adds up to a numbing 40 to 70 hours per week (or an average of 55 hours per week) spent in various mind-control practices.

RECRUITING TECHNIQUES USED BY CULTS

There are a variety of techniques used by cults to influence new recruits. They include:

Totally controlling the physical and psychological environment of members. This includes cutting them off from friends, family, and school.

Making members totally dependent upon the group for their physical survival and happiness.

Generating a fear of leaving the group. This can involve, for example, indoctrinating members into believing that they can never be happy outside the group or may become ill or die if they leave.

Placing members on a poor diet and providing inadequate health care, if any. Both of these techniques physically weaken members, thereby interfering with their ability to think clearly.

Forcing members to work long hours, with little time to rest or sleep. This technique deprives members of the necessary mental and physical energy to resist.

Controlling channels of communication by cutting members off from outside sources of information.

Manipulating language by assigning special meanings to words. This technique makes members feel as if they are part of an elite group.

Inducing trance-like states of mind that allow members to be easily influenced.

Forcing embarrassing public confessions of misbehavior that leave members vulnerable to emotional manipulation.

Tightly controlling time and activities and allowing little or no privacy. This technique robs members of whatever time they might otherwise have to think about or evaluate their commitment to the group.

DISCUSSION GUIDE TO *TICKET TO HEAVEN*

NOTE TO DISCUSSION LEADERS

Ticket to Heaven is a powerful film. Viewers may need some time after the video is played to express their feelings openly and formulate their thoughts. Allow them the freedom to do so. The questions below should be discussed in small groups after the video is played.

INTRODUCTION

Ticket to Heaven is the film adaptation of a book based on the actual experiences of a young schoolteacher from Canada who became involved in the Unification Church. The victim in this case happens to be Jewish, but the film has universal significance. What happened to David has happened to people of all faiths.

In the film we meet a disillusioned schoolteacher named David Kapell, who decides to get away from it all by visiting his old friend Karl in San Francisco. Upon his arrival, David is introduced by Karl to a number of attractive young people who belong to something called the Young Pioneer Center. Karl persuades David to join them for a weekend on the farm where they work—a weekend that turns into a nightmare.

While some students may find the story hard to believe, it is no more unbelievable than what followed the 1993 standoff between the followers of David Koresh and officers from the FBI and ATF during the siege of the Branch Davidian compound in Waco, Texas. Some students may even remember the 900 members of the People's Temple who committed suicide at the command of cult leader Jim Jones. Similarly, the first reports about the Holocaust—a deliberate campaign to exterminate millions of Jews, an entire people—were also incredible to many. However, the Jews, like many other peoples, know that the unthinkable can happen; indeed, the unthinkable *has* happened. Our historic memory thus makes us sensitive to totalitarianism in *any* form, especially when practiced in the name of religion.

The deceptive techniques and destructive life-style depicted in the film are characteristic of more than one modern cult movement. As the students watch, ask if they can spot the techniques used to attract young people and to keep them involved in these movements. Ask them to decide what they would have done at each step of the way if they had been David, David's friend, or one of his parents.

QUESTIONS FOR DISCUSSION

1. **What is the significance of the title *Ticket to Heaven*?**
   Destructive cults recruit followers and obtain financial contributions by fraudulent means, using sophisticated techniques to deceive, manipulate, and coerce potential members.

2. **What lies are told to gain money and converts?**
   In the film, a cult member secures donations by falsely telling others that he works for a Christian group that is raising money for a rehabilitation center. (Other cult groups employ similar techniques. For example, Hare Krishna devotees wear Santa Claus suits at Christmastime in order to deceive almsgivers into believing that they are making donations to another charity. Sometimes they also wear Western clothing and wigs to disguise their membership. They approach young teenagers, offering to sell them records by popular artists, though the records are actually for proselytizing listeners. Cult members have also been accused of playing con games, such as giving wrong amounts of change, stealing credit cards, and even assaulting individuals. Others have been accused of art scams, selling and smuggling drugs, and other illicit activities.)

   Karl and other members lie to David about the nature of the group. They tell him that the "Young Pioneers" are not part of a religion and that they are going to change the world by building a better society. (Interestingly, they have no programs to accomplish this noble objective. Instead their lives are spent performing demeaning jobs; they are often on the streets sell-ing flowers and gaining converts, who are then trained to do the same. The leader, who receives the money from these sales, is not accountable to anyone for how it is spent. All of these groups claim to be religions, which places them under the pro-tection of the First Amendment. Some groups, like Scientol-ogy, tell followers that they are alternate mental-health therapy groups while also claiming IRS tax-exempt status as religious institutions. Transcendental Meditation, which claims to be an educational group, has been declared by the courts to be a reli-gion because its rituals are based on Hindu ritual and the mantra chanted by followers is the name of a Hindu god.)

David lies to his parents as the first step in breaking commu-nication with his family. (Destructive cults typically encourage their members to break all ties with the outside world, espe-cially their parents. By labeling everyone outside the group an agent of Satan, including members' close relatives, the cult group can offer itself as a substitute family.)

David also lies to his friend Larry—the same way Karl has lied to David—in order to recruit him as a new member.

3. **How are the lies justified?**
One justification or excuse is offered by the flower seller: "It's only Satan's money we are taking. If that man were dying in a fire, wouldn't you do anything to save him? Well, he is dying! And we've just sold him a ticket to heaven." (Destructive cults all operate according to the same principle—the end justifies the means. This runs contrary to legitimate religious systems. This principle, which is called "Heavenly Deception" in the Unification Church and "Transcendental Trickery" in Hare Krishna, functions as an excuse for deceptive practices. The man mentioned by the flower seller is not dying. He is being cheated out of making an informed choice about his donation, just as David was denied the opportunity to make a similar choice about his new religion.)

Because each cult considers itself to be the only "true" religion, everyone outside it is regarded as an agent of Satan who may be lied to and harassed in order to enhance or protect the group. Members of some groups are even trained to commit suicide or murder, if necessary (as is depicted in the film). For example, on February 18, 1982, the *Kansas City Star* reported that former members of The Way International "say without hesitation that they gladly would have killed anyone, including their own parents," if their leader had asked. The leadership of Synanon was found guilty of attempted murder of an attorney who won a lawsuit against the group. Some groups like the Branch Davidians, MOVE, The Way International, and Hare Krishna have stockpiled large caches of weapons on their premises. Many of these groups see themselves as above the law and have been charged with violations of immigration, banking, currency, arms control laws, as well as the obstruction of justice and income tax evasion.

4. **What techniques are used to attract David and keep him involved with the "Young Pioneers"?**
Smiling Faces: The group's offer of unconditional friendship, instant community, and instant purpose appeals to the confused and aimless young man who has lost the two most important people in his life: his grandfather and his girlfriend. The offer of certainty in an uncertain world is also appealing.

Appeal to Idealism: The group pretends to be building a better world. Other groups present themselves as the answer to the hypocrisy of traditional religious systems, the antidote to the materialism in the world, or the only way to help a person build a better self. Yet the practices of these destructive cults are more hypocritical, more materialistic, and more destructive of the personality than the systems they seek to replace. The songs they sing in the film ("Blowing in the Wind," "When the Red Red Robin Comes Bob Bob Bobbing Along," and "Amazing Grace") all appeal to a naive, simplistic approach to resolving the problems of the world.

Mind-Stilling Activities: The childish chant "Chooch-a-

Chooch" and the childish group games and frenetic exercises recreate a childlike enthusiasm and attachment to the group that exhaust a person until he or she is too tired to think. Cults use a variety of self-hypnotic rituals to prevent prospective converts from thinking clearly. These rituals include intense meditation, chanting, speaking in tongues, and "auditing sessions" or "centering" on the leader's teachings.

Buddy System: You are never left alone. In the film, for example, David is followed to the bathroom by a male buddy who is assigned to follow him wherever he goes. When he rejects his buddy's companionship and tries to find time and space alone, he is immediately joined by attractive young women who grab his hands to talk with him. When he tries to run away, he is surrounded by the group.

Peer Pressure: David is surrounded by attractive girls who encourage him to stay by flirting with him. Destructive cults typically use the possibility or prohibition of sexual relationships to approach recruits and encourage their interest in the group. When David tries to touch the girl sitting next to him, for example, he is informed that such contact is forbidden out of respect for women. All contact between men and women is controlled by the leader of the group. In most cases, contact is forbidden unless the group leader has chosen a marriage partner for you. In a few cults, such as The Children of God, also known as The Family of Love, the leader forces female members to engage in sexual relationships. As "fishers of men" (i.e., prostitutes), female members use sex as a tool for gaining new male members. Women are systematically used and abused in most of these movements. Two thousand couples, for example, actually allowed the Reverend Moon to select their mates for them (that is, "marry" people they had met but two days before) only to be separated from them and forced to work on separate continents.

Group Confession-Sharing: David, along with other members of the group, is encouraged to reveal his innermost thoughts and discuss those things of which he is most ashamed. (Destructive cults use this technique to learn a person's weaknesses so that the person can be more easily manipulated. In the film, Larry almost succumbs to the group's flattery when they ask him to perform for them. Many critics claim that some groups also use this information for blackmail. This technique breaks down psychological barriers, rendering members dependent upon the group.)

Love-Bombing: The group "bombs with love" David and later Larry by constantly telling them how great they are. (Destructive cults use love as a weapon, offering prospective recruits instant love, friendship, and community, as long as they obey the leader's rules without question.)

Guilt: When David eats "forbidden food," he literally cannot stomach it because he feels so guilty. (Destructive cults exploit the guilt they create by convincing members that the only way to alleviate that guilt is to devote all their time and donate all their money to the leader.)

Isolation: The "farm" is in an isolated area, surrounded by barbed wire. David and the others are, therefore, completely dependent on the group for transportation. They are also cut off from communication with the outside world. They have no money or possessions, except for the clothes on their backs; their phone calls are monitored and their letters read. All communication with the outside world has, in effect, been cut off. (This pattern is common among cults. In those that do permit participants to hold jobs in the outside community, most of the members' earnings go to the group. They spend all their time away from the job with the group.)

5. **In the movie, David is recruited by a friend and then recruits another friend. Do you know anyone who was recruited to join a cult? How was it done?**

Cults recruit in subtly deceptive ways. The initial approach is always the "Smiling Face," when a person is alone. At that time the cult may offer something at no cost or an invitation to any of the following: a free social event; a Sunday feast; a dinner; a rock concert; a lecture; a coffee house entertainment; free yoga lessons; free meditation lessons; a free personality test; "non-denominational" Bible lessons, and so forth. The indoctrination process of some cults like Scientology, The Way International, and Divine Light Mission depends on frequent contact over a longer period of time and is less immediate than that of the Unification Church, Hare Krishna, and others.

6. **Does David know what the life-style of the group is when he first comes to the compound? What does the opening scene in the van tell you about the life-style?**
   Sleep: In the opening scene members chant "Stay Awake" constantly because they are so tired they keep falling asleep. (Destructive cults deliberately keep people working physically hard for long hours. Members frequently get as little as three to four hours of sleep a night.)

   Work: Work is generally of the demeaning sort like David's (i.e., selling flowers on the street to gain converts). Cult members often work 18 hours a day or until a quota has been met (estimated to be approximately $150 a day per person, although some bring in much more). Members sometimes work the same number of hours in specific businesses run by cult groups, with all of their earnings going to the group.

   Food: How much weight do you estimate David lost after just a few weeks in the group? Why? What kind of food did he get? How much? (Destructive cults deliberately keep members on a low-protein diet without enough calories. The combination of long work hours with little sleep and not enough food makes members too tired to think.)

   Education: Is David, a teacher, encouraged to learn or discouraged from learning anything other than the leader's teachings? (Destructive cults view outside teachings as dangerous, even Satanic. College students are encouraged to drop out of school in order to spend all their time working for the leader. Thinking is viewed as the enemy. Members are urged, if not coerced, to stop thinking so they can't question the leader.) Is David fully acquainted with the leader's writings? (The deprogramming scenes indicate he actually does not know them because he has not read the "Sacred Scriptures.")

Medical Care: In the restaurant scene when David and his companions meet Larry, Larry notices that David has such a bad case of poison ivy that his companions have to cut his food for him. Members lie and tell Larry that David is being treated by a doctor. (Most destructive cults provide no medical care for members. Illness is instead treated as a sign of disbelief. The "cure" is to work harder, pray and chant more hours, sleep less, and so on in order to prove one's devotion to the leader. Some members have died as a result of lack of medical treatment. This lack of care applies even to those who come into the group with a known illness, such as diabetes, that requires constant medication.)

7. **How does the life-style affect members? What changes did you see in David?**
   There is often a sudden change from independent to dependent behavior patterns, extreme signs of which include a zombie-like stare and the mental inability to evaluate new information.

8. **Do you think that when David entered the group, he converted to this new religion of his own free will? Do you think he remained in the group of his own free will? Was he free to leave at any time?**

9. **In your opinion, what freedoms, if any, were denied David while he was in the group?**

10. **What would you have done if you were David's parent? If you were David's friend? Would you risk imprisonment to save him?**

11. **What was the purpose of deprogramming? What freedoms, if any, were denied David in the process? What**

lies were told to get David away from the group? How are such lies justified? Can this be placed in the category of saving a life?

Deprogramming is a controversial solution to which desperate parents resort in order to rescue their children from these movements. In this case David was kidnapped and denied the freedom to leave the premises. In other cases, deprogramming is voluntary.

12. **Why did David's parents think deprogramming was necessary?**

    The purpose of deprogramming is to challenge the person who has become involved with a cult to think, so that he or she can make an informed choice. In the process, for example, David discovers that he has not even read the leader's teachings. He knows only as much as he has been told, has had no opportunity to evaluate the information, and never really knew the beliefs or practices that defined his membership in the group. The breaking point is his discovery of the hypocrisy of the leader, who was making money from munitions plants.

13. **What answers do the deprogrammers have for David?**

    None. The answer is that David must find the answers for himself. No one can find them for him. *There are no easy answers, no instant solutions to life's problems.* Reaching maturity is a process of making choices and taking responsibility for the consequences of those choices.

14. **At the end, does it look as if David will stay with his family and friends or will he be tempted to return to "Young Pioneers"?**

15. **Was there anything left out of the movie?**

    There is no indication of physical abuse, assault, beatings, or bizarre punishments of members.

16. **What should or can you do to prevent this from happening to you and to others?**

    Before going away with or joining an unknown group, investigate it. It's never too late to join, but it may be too late to leave. Check with your rabbi; call the Cult Hotline/Crisis Clinic (Jewish Board of Family and Children's Services of New York) at 212-860-8533 or the Cult Clinic (Jewish Family Service of Los Angeles) at 213-852-1234, extension 1650.

17. **How can you resist peer pressure to engage in harmful activities (such as smoking, drinking, marijuana, drugs, pills, petty vandalism, harassing other teenagers, etc.)? What have you been pressured into trying with a group your own age that you might not have done on your own? Why?**

18. **How are the conclaves, shut-ins, and weekend retreats that you attend different from the cult experience?**

    You know where you are going (if you don't, you should be able to ask and receive a satisfactory answer) and who is sponsoring the event. You have access to communication with friends and family and you can leave if you want. You are encouraged to think and to question authority; you get plenty of food; you have time to be by yourself, socialize, or talk to anyone—including the outside world. You are also encouraged to get enough sleep, read anything you want, and take private time if you want it. You also know that you will be going home when the weekend is over.

Why Jews Join Cults

Goals
- To realize that Jews are often involved in cults and cult-like groups.
- To explore the reasons Jews become involved in these groups.
- To determine the way in which the Jewish community may respond to the involvement of Jews in these groups.

Objectives
Students will be able to:
- State facts about the involvement of Jews in cults and cult-like groups.
- List the signals that indicate a person is likely to become involved in a cult.
- Describe the factors that led to the involvement (and subsequent noninvolvement) of the individuals in *You Can Go Home Again.*
- Decide on the type of advice to give Jewish professionals who deal with cult members and potential recruits.
- Determine the role the Jewish community should play in combating the participation of Jews in cults.

Materials
Video: *You Can Go Home Again*, 47 mins. (See Appendix I.)

Activities
1. Ask the students to answer the following questions:
   - Do you think Jews are involved in cults or cult-like groups in a greater percentage than other people? Why or why not?
   - What kind of Jewish person do you think gets involved in a cult?
   - Do Jews have the same vulnerability points as others?
2. View the video *You Can Go Home Again*.
3. Make a graph on the board, listing the names of the individuals shown in the film at the top of the columns. Using the questions below, review each person's story with the students. Then write a few words in each column about each individual's experience. (You may also want to use questions from previous sessions as a guide.)
   - Was the individual recruited into the group under false pretenses (i.e., not told the true nature of the group)?
   - Was the individual forced to engage in sexual activity?
   - List the reasons various people said they got involved with cults.
   - Who or what helped them get out?
   - Did ex-members see these experiences as harmful, destructive, or painful? Why or why not?
   - Do you think the experience affected them permanently? In what way?
4. Use the questions below as a way to teach students that these ex-cult members are still *real people*, no different from any of the Jewish people in their synagogues or communities. Ask the students:
   - Do they remind you of anyone you know?
   - Do you know anyone who has been involved in a cult?
   - What were the factors that led to his or her involvement in a cult?

5. These questions focus the discussion on the involvement of Jews in cults. Ask the students:
   - Why do Jews get involved in cults?
   - Did their Jewish background affect their experience or their reasons for joining the cult in the first place?
   - Do you think the number of Jews in cults is lower or higher than the average in America? (It is actually much higher. Even though less than 3% of the American population identifies with Judaism, it is possible that as many as 12% of cult members are Jewish. Furthermore, Eastern or Hindu-based groups seem to attract Jews most; as many as 25–30% of their members are Jews.[1] This figure includes the Divine Light Mission, Hare Krishna, Muktanada, Rajneesh, and Transcendental Meditation.)
   - Do you have any explanations for this phenomenon?
   - Do you think the rabbi in the video handled the situation well? What might he have done better? Do you think the people being interviewed felt comfortable talking to him? What advice might you give him or any other Jewish professional in dealing with members or potential members of cults? (If there is time, have students role-play this scenario.)
   - Should the involvement of Jews in cults be an issue the Jewish community should deal with in a more aggressive manner? In what way?
   - Can one belong to a cult and still be Jewish? Are there limits to which cults one might belong?
6. Optional: Invite an ex-cult member to the class to share his or her experiences with the students. (This individual should be Jewish.) The students should be encouraged to ask questions of the ex-cult member. The teacher may want to pose some of the following questions first in order to stimulate further questions from the students:

---

1. See, for example, Roger Kametz, *The Jew in the Lotus: A Poet's Rediscovery of Jewish Identity in Buddhist India* (San Francisco: Harper & Row, 1994).

- What was happening in the ex-cult member's life at the time he or she encountered the cult?
- How did the ex-cult member explain (to himself or herself) what was going on?
- What did the ex-cult member think when the cult he or she had joined prohibited all family contacts?
- Did the ex-cult member have a positive relationship with Judaism?
- Why do you (the students) think the ex-cult member became involved with that particular group?

7. Optional Homework: Divide the class into several groups. Each group should outline a two-hour program to be implemented in the Jewish community (synagogue, community center, general community, etc.) that deals with the issue of cults. The program should focus on the most important aspect of the issue from the point of view of the Jewish community.

Who Recruits and Why?

Goals

- To experience how it feels to convince another person to join a group.
- To experience how it feels to be recruited to join a group.
- To understand why you might want a friend to join your group (or vice versa).
- To be aware of those personality traits common to cult leaders.

Objectives

Students will be able to:

- State the reasons why they might want a friend to join their group (or their friend might want them to join a particular group).
- List the benefits of recruiting someone to join a group.
- State the personality traits common to cult leaders.

Materials

1. Handout: "Group #1: Rules to Live By" (p. 68).
2. Handout: "Group #2: Rules to Live By" (p. 69).
3. Optional: Pictures of various cult leaders to place on the wall, such as the Reverend Sun Myung Moon, David Koresh, Bhag-

wan Shree Rajneesh, Jim Jones, L. Ron Hubbard, Lyndon LaRouche, etc.

4. A copy of *Combatting Cult Mind Control* by Steven Hassan and information packets on cults from the American Family Foundation. (See Appendix I.)

Activities

1. Divide the class into two groups. Give each group a copy of "Rules to Live By." Tell each group that this set of rules is the key to happiness and successful living and that group members should pretend to believe that their lives have changed dramatically since discovering these rules. Have each group pick one representative (or two) to convince a member of the other group of the value of these rules. The representative may use whatever approach or technique works. Repeat the exercise several times with different students from each group. Allow no more than five minutes per round, so more students may participate. Bring the groups back together and ask them the following questions:

   • Is there anything that has given greater meaning and direction to your life (religion, participation in a sport or hobby, a group of friends)? Or in the life of someone you know?

   • What happens when you believe very strongly in something? Do you want to share your knowledge or understanding with someone else? Why?

   • How might you feel if you fervently believed your group, knowledge, or understanding would benefit someone else who seems to be having a particularly difficult time? How would you feel if that person resisted help?

2. Discuss the reasons cult followers recruit others.

   a. Have students recall the movie *The Wave* and ask them the following questions:

      • Why did the students who were members/followers begin to try to encourage other students to join their group?

      • How did they do so?

- Did they personally benefit from others' joining? Did the group benefit? In what ways, if they did?

b. Have the students draw up a list of "benefits" a recruiter ostensibly derives from recruiting others. Use the following list as a guide:

- Excitement that the group is gaining in popularity.
- Excitement that the purposes of the group are more likely to be fulfilled by increasing the number of members who can "spread the word" or "live the truth."
- Increased prestige within the group for bringing in new members, including possibly a higher status or rank within the group.
- Material rewards for bringing in new members (as well as winning the favor of the leader).
- Boosting of ego from sense of success.

c. After they consider these benefits, discuss with the students why a cult member might feel compelled to recruit new members. Offer as possible answers:

- He or she has been brainwashed into believing that this is what he or she *must* do; he or she no longer questions whether this behavior is right or not.
- He or she has been physically and/or emotionally threatened or abused and, therefore, does as he or she is told.

3. Discuss the reasons cult leaders recruit followers.

a. If you have pictures of the cult leaders, place them on the wall and go over their names and the cults they lead with the students.

b. Again have the students recall the teacher in the movie *The Wave* and ask them the following questions about him:

- How did he change over the course of his experiment?
- Why did he want more recruits?
- Do you think that those who become cult leaders have common personality traits? What are they?

c. With the students draw up a list of personality traits common to cult leaders. Use the following list as a guide:

- Authoritarian personalities.
- Need to dominate others.
- Need for material gain at recruits' expense.
- Sadistic tendencies that feed on others' masochistic tendencies.
- Claim to have special status, power, secret knowledge, or special relationship with a higher power.

4. Optional Homework: Have each student choose a cult leader to research and report on at the next class session.

GROUP #1: RULES TO LIVE BY

1. Being organized in life will bring you greater prestige and honor from those around you. The new record-keeper that the group has manufactured is the surest, easiest way to stay organized.

2. Being prompt with your meetings and appointments will win you the respect of your classmates. The new record-keeper will ensure that you remember your appointments and have ample time to get to them.

3. Planning out each day will give you greater control in your life. The record-keeper provides you with a convenient system for planning and thinking through each day.

4. Reviewing and evaluating each day will give you a sense of peace and self-satisfaction. The record-keeper has a built-in means to review and evaluate the day's events.

5. Setting priorities and recording them in the daily record-keeper will keep you focused and insure that you will be more content with your life.

GROUP #2: RULES TO LIVE BY

1. The key to happiness is simplicity. One must live as simple a life as possible.

2. One should let go of all anger and resentment. If one feels those emotions surfacing, one should take three deep breaths and let the emotions disappear on the exhalation.

3. When one feels any unpleasant emotions, one should recite a word or phrase over and over again. The word "shalom" works well for this.

4. One should always approach another with love and understanding in one's heart. Even if someone does something that might cause anger or hurt, it is best to forgive that person and embrace him or her with compassion.

Techniques of Recruitment

Goals

- To witness the various techniques cults use to recruit individuals, including pressure (high-pressure sales technique) manipulation (flirting, exacerbating a recruit's sense of guilt or uncertainty); and deception (evading the truth or outright lying).
- To teach some methods for responding to the manipulative, deceptive, and high-pressure recruiting techniques used by cults.

Objectives

Students will be able to:

- Identify manipulative practices as they are being used.
- Resist pressure tactics until the students are in a place where they can think more clearly and more objectively.
- Determine if they are getting the information they need in order to make a sound decision.

Materials

1. Handout: "Recruitment Scenario #1" (pp. 74–75).
2. Handout: "Recruitment Scenario #2" (pp. 76–77). [1]

1. Both handouts are excerpted and adapted from the video *Cults: Saying 'No' Under Pressure*. (See Appendix I.)

Activities

1. Briefly review last session. (Allow time for student presentations on the various cult leaders if the optional homework was assigned and completed.)

2. Dramatize recruitment techniques. In "Recruitment Scenario #1" students witness a "typical" conversation between a cult recruiter and a student whom she has carefully selected for recruitment. The conversation can take place in a library or student lounge. The cult recruiter, an attractive young woman named Jennifer, enters the room and spots Sam, a potential recruit, sitting at a table alone, reading a book and studying some notes. In this first dramatization, the teacher may want to play the part of Jennifer. (Please note that the roles are not gender specific; the recruiter is just as likely to be a male student and the recruit a female.) Following the dramatization, ask the students to respond to the following questions:

   - Who is Jennifer? Is she a student at the school? Do we know for sure?
   - How did Jennifer win Sam's interest? How many times did she repeat his name? How do you think her repetition of Sam's name made him feel? How might you have felt if an attractive person were showing you this kind of attention?
   - What subtle message does Jennifer try to convey to Sam (regarding her interest in him)?
   - Why does Jennifer insist that Sam come that very night? How do you think her insistence made Sam feel? How do you respond when people are insistent, especially in a "friendly" or "loving" way? Share some examples from your own life when you've experienced this. How did you respond?
   - If Sam passed up the opportunity to join the group that evening, what other options were available to him? How did Jennifer convey this? How do you feel when you think you might miss out on something that sounds exciting or fun?
   - How does Jennifer contrast the various possibilities in Sam's

life (helping to improve the world versus building up his career; being a good person versus being a selfish person)?

- Does Jennifer work on Sam's feelings of guilt? Do you think she did this intentionally?
- Why didn't Jennifer say the name of the group? Why did she say that it was a school club?
- Who was controlling the conversation between Jennifer and Sam? Do you think Sam was able to make clear decisions about what he wanted to do? Why or why not?

3. Have the students generate a list of the techniques Jennifer used to win Sam's interest. Use the following list as a guide:
   - Friendly demeanor, smiling face
   - Playing on a person's desire to be loved and accepted (a technique known as "love-bombing")
   - Flirting
   - Flattery
   - Appeal to idealism
   - Pretense of friendship
   - Invitation to free social event
   - Deception
   - Pressure
   - Playing on guilt or remorse
   - Discouraging questions or critical thought

4. Explain to the students that they will now try an exercise that will help them recognize and effectively respond to manipulative, deceptive, and high-pressure tactics. They will replay the same scenario, this time using "Recruitment Scenario #2." Again, the teacher may want to play the part of Jennifer. Ask students to note the differences between Sam's responses and Jennifer's reactions to them. Alternatively, play "freeze" and have students jump into the scenario in both Jennifer's and Sam's parts. Or have the students create their own recruitment scenario.

5. Ask the students:
   - When and how did Sam's responses change?
   - What do you think he was feeling?
   - How did Jennifer respond to his different tone of voice?

RECRUITMENT SCENARIO #1

Jennifer: *(Looking over shoulder of student sitting at a table and noting the title of the book he's reading)* Hey, I took that class last year. It's very hard. Can you believe how much work there is for just that class? It really puts you under a lot of pressure.

Sam: Yeah, I'm swamped.

Jennifer: School is just hard to deal with sometimes.

Sam: No kidding.

Jennifer: *(Sits down at the table across from Sam)* I'm Jennifer. What's your name?

Sam: Sam.

Jennifer: Sam, I can tell that you're concerned about important issues. *(Sam nods.)* I belong to a discussion group that talks about these things. We're getting together tonight, Sam. I'd like to invite you to come with me!

Sam: Maybe some other time. I have a lot of work to do for this class.

Jennifer: Come on—what's one night out of your life? We discuss politics and how to improve the world.

Sam: Yeah, it sure is a mess. But right now I don't have much time to worry about it. My parents are nagging me to get good grades. They want me to get a good job and be a big success, you know?

Jennifer: So many people are starving and homeless, Sam! You mean you'd rather go out and make money than help improve the world?

Sam: *(Weakly)* Well, no.

Jennifer: *(Softening the tone of her voice)* We have a lot of fun, too. We always have a party afterwards, with great food. *(She pauses and looks into Sam's eyes.)* And I'd really like to get to know you better, Sam. *(Sam, responding to the eye contact, begins to look interested. Jennifer notices this.)* You should come.

We really need great people like you in our group, Sam. I'll take you.

Sam: A party would be fun. I could use a break.

Jennifer: Great! I'm glad you're coming! I can't wait for my friends to meet you. They're going to love you, Sam.

Sam: Is this a school club?

Jennifer: *(Hesitantly)* Yes.

Sam: What's it called?

Jennifer: *(With greater assurance)* We don't have a name. We're just a group of people who care about what's really important and want to make the world a better place.

RECRUITMENT SCENARIO #2

Jennifer: *(Looking over shoulder of student sitting at a table and noting the title of the book he's reading)* Hey, I took that class last year. It's very hard. Can you believe how much work there is for just that class? It really puts you under a lot of pressure.

Sam: Yeah, I'm swamped.

Jennifer: School is just hard to deal with sometimes.

Sam: No kidding.

Jennifer: *(Sits down at the table across from Sam)* I'm Jennifer. What's your name?

Sam: Sam.

Jennifer: Sam, I can tell that you're concerned about important issues. *(Sam nods.)* I belong to a discussion group that talks about these things. We're getting together tonight, Sam. I'd like to invite you to come with me!

Sam: Maybe some other time. I have a lot of work to do for this class.

Jennifer: Come on—what's one night out of your life? We discuss politics and how to improve the world.

Sam: Yeah, it sure is a mess. But right now I don't have much time to worry about it. My parents are nagging me to get good grades. They want me to get a good job and be a big success, you know?

Jennifer: So many people are starving and homeless, Sam! You mean you'd rather go out and make money than help improve the world?

Sam: I don't think it's "either/or." I can help people and still have a good career. I'd donate money and do volunteer work in my spare time.

Jennifer: *(Softening the tone of her voice)* We have a lot of fun, too. We always have a party afterwards, with great food. *(She* *pauses and looks into Sam's eyes.)* And I'd really like to get to know you better, Sam.

Sam: *(Resistantly)* Well, I hope you have a good time. But I need to stay home tonight.

Jennifer: We really need great people like you in our group, Sam. We can go together.

Sam: *(Cautiously and even a little resentfully)* Thanks, but I just don't have time. By the way, is this a school club? What's it called?

Jennifer: We don't really have a name. We're just a group of people who care about what's really important and want to make the world a better place.

Sam: If it's not an official school club, then I'm not interested. Look, it's been nice talking to you, but I need to get back to my work now. *(Firmly)* Good-bye.

The Development of the Messianic Idea and the Jewish Position on Jesus

Goals

- To understand where the concept of a Messiah comes from.
- To understand the social and historical background of Judaism during the first century C.E. by learning about the Jewish groups that existed during this time, their respective positions in and toward Judaism, and their relations with the Roman government.
- To learn what Jews believe about Jesus.
- To be aware that many Christian teachings are, in fact, Jewish in origin.

Objectives

Students will be able to:

- Provide a definition and history of the word "Messiah."
- Briefly state the historical environment in which Judaism existed during the first century C.E.
- State the philosophies and ways of life of the Sadducees, Pharisees, Zealots, and Essenes.
- State two facts that Jews believe about Jesus.
- Identify the origin of several Christian teachings.

Materials

1. Handout: "Primary Jewish Groups during the First Century C.E. " (pp. 83–84).[1]
2. Handout: "What Jews Believe about Jesus" (p. 85).

Activities

1. Start the session by asking students:
   - If there were a person or thing that could save you from your greatest problems, what would you ask that person or thing to do? (Students may joke about this. But, after they have stopped, ask them to think seriously and write down their answers to this question and these that follow.)
   - Today, if the Jewish people could ask that person or thing to save them from its greatest problems, what might the Jewish people ask?
   - What might the Jewish people have asked for 50 years ago? 200 years ago? 2,000 years ago?
2. Spend a few minutes reviewing the students' responses to these questions. Put the answers on the board in columns labeled: "Today," "50 Years Ago," "200 Years Ago," and "2,000 Years Ago." Then give the following explanation:

   During the period of the First Temple, the Davidic dynasty was ruled by monarchs, or anointed kings. The people believed that the descendants of King David would always reign in Jerusalem. After the collapse of the Davidic dynasty, the Jews were exiled from their land to Babylon. Separated from their sacred sites, they were unable to worship as they had in the past. This left them distraught and longing for the day when a descendant of David would sit upon the throne in Jerusalem. They hoped for a leader who would restore them to their former greatness and independence in their homeland. When that time came, the Temple would be rebuilt and the sacrifices reinstituted.

   In Hebrew, the term used for a man consecrated to high office (i.e., kings and priests) was *mashiach*, which meant

---

1. Adapted from *Missionary and Cult Movements*, pp. 1–2.

"anointed one." This was because in those days there was a ceremony in which special benedictions were said and oil was poured on the head of such an individual. In biblical times, the *mashiach*, it was believed, was to be a human descendant of David. It was into this setting that Jesus was born and lived. The Hebrew word *mashiach* was later translated into the Greek *messiah*. Jesus Christ means "Jesus the Messiah."

3. Briefly review the history of the Jews who lived in the first century C.E., explaining to students the various religious sects that existed at the time of Jesus:

    At the beginning of the common era, when Roman rule was oppressive, Jews were severely restricted. Poverty was rampant, and what little possessions Jews did have were heavily taxed by Rome. Jews were arrested and killed with little or no reason. Because the people had so little hope, it is not surprising that they should look during this time for someone to "save" them. People cried out for their leaders to help them. Then, as now, there were different solutions offered by different Jewish political parties, all of which were religiously based.[2]

4. Divide the class into four groups and give each group a copy of "Primary Jewish Groups during the First Century C.E." Assign a first-century Jewish group to each group in class. Now, to help students understand the sociological context in which Jesus lived, have each group prepare a dramatization, "commercial," or "infomercial" of its philosophy and way of life.

5. Do the following activity with the students.

    a. Show various pictures of Moses from different books. Ask the students:
       • Do all of these look alike?
       • Which is the "true" Moses?

    b. Then show pictures of Jesus from different books.
       • Do all of these look alike?
       • Which is the "true" Jesus?

---

2. Ibid.

c. Go over with students the following explanation:

As with Moses, the historical validity of Jesus' story is uncertain. There are no writings about Jesus found in any historical documents from his own time. The only writings we know that concern Jesus of Nazareth are found in the New Testament, which is a religious document, a document of faith. Scholars believe that various fraudulent statements were later added to Josephus (a historian of the period) and to the Talmud concerning Jesus.

6. Go over with students the following facts about Jesus and the brief explanation of the Jewish attitude toward him:

Jesus was probably born approximately 6 B.C.E. and died approximately 30 C.E. He was a contemporary, therefore, of some of the great rabbis of Jewish tradition. It is, therefore, important to understand Jesus in the context of the culture in which he lived.

Jesus' teachings should not be compared with the writings found in the Old Testament but with mishnaic and midrashic writings. These writings were products of the same era as the New Testament.

Jesus is credited with ideas and teachings that were in common use at that time. Many note that Jesus is said to have spoken in parables. This is like the writings of the *Mishnah* and the Midrash, many parts of which are also written in the form of parables. The parable was one of the most commonly used teaching tools in the first century C.E. Many of Jesus' teachings are similar to well-known Jewish teachings, such as Jesus' statement: "Do unto others as you would have them do unto you." Compare it, for example, with a statement by Hillel, the great first-century rabbi, who said: "What is hateful to you do not do to your neighbor." (*Shabbat* 31a) And this isn't all. There are other sayings credited to Jesus that can be found in Jewish literature.

7. Ask students to decide where the following statements come from:
   - "Salt of the earth." (*Mishnah*)
   - "With what measure you mete, it shall be measured to your gain." (Midrash)
   - "If you forgive men their trespass, your Father in heaven will also forgive you." (Midrash)
   - "Give to him that asks of you, and from him that would borrow of you do not turn him away." (Midrash)
8. Ask students to share what they think Jews believe about Jesus. Then hand out "What Jews Believe about Jesus." Have the students use the handout to explain their position and beliefs as Jews; ask them to write a letter to a friend who has been sharing with them his or her deep belief in Jesus.

PRIMARY JEWISH GROUPS
DURING THE FIRST CENTURY C.E.

SADDUCEES

The Sadducees were a conservative priestly class. They were an aristocratic group whose members inherited their leadership positions based on their births. They were also wealthy and cooperated with Rome in governing the Jews. They believed in a strict, literal interpretation of Torah. They also believed that the legacy of Torah laws regarding sacrifice, the Temple cult, and so on were the sources of the Sadducees' own authority and wealth.

PHARISEES

The Pharisees were liberals, most of whom were unhappy with Roman rule but felt that it was useless for the people to rise against Rome because they would be crushed. Leaders were scribes and scholars who studied and interpreted the Torah. Leadership was based on learning and character. They believed in interpreting the Torah to meet the needs of the times. They carefully observed ritual and fostered democracy by insisting on education in Torah for *all* boys.

The Pharisees believed that people should obey Roman law and rely on God, who would send a Messiah, a redeemer, out of the house of David to overthrow the oppressors. They believed that once this Messiah came, all could live in a just society of peace. The Pharisees also believed in resurrection.

ZEALOTS

The Zealots were militant Pharisees. They wanted to overthrow Rome and felt that every Jew must join in the uprising because no Jew could be loyal to both God and the emperor. *Sicarii*, "dagger men," were a terrorist element among the Zealots. They killed Jews without trial and urged the burning of the granaries because they belonged to wealthy Jews. Their motto was: "No God, but *Yahweh*; no tax, but to the Temple; no friend, but the Zealot." Roman authorities viewed the Zealots as political subversives and arrested leaders of the group on charges of treason.

ESSENES

The Essenes were a religious group that retreated from society to live communally. They established Qumran, a monastery-like retreat on the edge of the Dead Sea. They were very strict observers of the pharisaic tradition who felt that in order to live rightly they must live by themselves away from the rest of society. One could not automatically become a member of Qumran but had to serve a probationary period. In Qumran, there was no private ownership. Essenes dressed simply, in plain white linen garments, and were vegetarian. Some were celibate. They washed frequently in order to be clean and pure and knew how to heal the sick using herbs and plants. They were in favor of keeping the peace and cooperating with Rome because the Romans could not be overthrown until the Messiah appeared.

WHAT JEWS BELIEVE ABOUT JESUS

1. Jesus was not a divine being. Jesus was a child of God in the way that we are all children of God.

2. God does not assume a physical form. This concept is supported by the biblical prohibition against our worshiping any physical likeness of God. This prohibition is described in Deuteronomy 4:15–16: "For your own sake, therefore, be most careful—since you saw no shape when *Adonai* your God spoke to you at Horeb out of the fire—not to act wickedly and make for yourselves a sculptured image in any likeness whatever: the form of a man or a woman." It is repeated in Deuteronomy 5:8–9: "You shall not make for yourself a sculptured image, any likeness of what is in the heavens above, or on the earth below, or in the waters below the earth. You shall not bow down to them or serve them."

3. God transcends time and space. This is contrary to the concept of the Trinity, in which God is represented by three distinct aspects: the Father, Son, and Holy Ghost. In the Son, according to Christianity, God became physically incarnate as Jesus Christ.

4. No one serves as an intermediary between human beings and God (even symbolically).

5. No one can provide vicarious atonement for another person; Jesus does not save us from our sins. According to Christianity, sin was brought into the world because Adam and Eve ate the forbidden apple in the Garden of Eden. From that moment on, all people were born into sin. In Judaism, there is no concept of original sin. According to Judaism, the story of Adam and Eve is not about sin but the free choice human beings make between good or evil. In terms of atoning for sin, Christians believe Jesus is the way to salvation. His sacrifice (on the cross) washed away all human sin. Jews believe that repentance and good deeds are the ways to salvation. We each must atone for our own misdeeds.

How to Respond to Christian Missionaries and the Proof Texts They Use

Goals

- To observe the dynamic that is created when a Jewish person is approached by a Christian missionary.
- To understand some of the factors that motivate missionaries to convert Jews and to understand some of the cult-like techniques employed.
- To realize that arguing theology and philosophy with a missionary is not a productive response.
- To become familiar with the proof texts most often cited by Christian missionaries and to understand some of the textual nuances that give rise to different interpretations.
- To become familiar with the Jewish interpretation of those texts.

Objectives

Students will be able to:

- Identify the deceptive practices and techniques used by those trying to convert or proselytize them.
- Identify their own emotional reactions to such efforts.
- Describe the dynamic between a missionizing Christian, Jew for

Jesus, or Messianic Jew and the Jew who has been targeted.
- Respond calmly and nondefensively if approached by a missionary who wants to "prove" the "truth" through the use of texts.
- Identify the various reasons Jews interpret certain prooftexts differently from the way Christians do.

Materials

1. Handout: Jews for Jesus materials: "How to Witness Effectively to the Jews" (p. 90), "Jews for Jesus: Strategy and Tactics" (p. 91), and "Jews for Jesus: A Confidential Report" (p. 92).[1]
2. Handout: "Two Proof Texts Used by Missionaries" (pp. 93–94).
3. Handout: "Responding to Christian Recruiters" (pp. 95–109).

Activities

1. Hand out copies of "How to Witness Effectively to the Jews." Explain to the students that for centuries up until the present, Christian missionaries have approached Jews in an attempt to share their feelings about Jesus. Many missionaries feel it is their religious duty to "witness" to Jews about Jesus. (Witnessing here means to proclaim one's faith about Jesus to another.) Some of the fundamentalist Christian, Hebrew Christian, and Messianic Jewish missionary groups who target Jews include Jews for Jesus, Chosen People Ministries, Messianic Vision, Assemblies of God, Slavic Gospel Association, and Messianic Jewish Movement International.
2. Ask the students:
   - Why do you think some Christians and even some Jews who have accepted Jesus feel compelled to "witness" to Jews?
   - Do you think they have a right to do so? Does it bother you that they do so at all? Why or why not?

---

1. This material has been taken from *Refuting Christian Missionaries: Teaching Materials and Facilitator's Guide* by the Jewish Community Task Force on Missionary Activities of the Synagogue Council of Massachusetts.

3. Hand out copies of "Jews for Jesus: Strategy and Tactics" (p. 91) and "Jews for Jesus: A Confidential Report" (p. 92) and ask students:
   - Is there anything deceptive about their techniques, methods, or approach? If so, what is it?
   - What do you feel when you read through this material? How do you feel knowing that there are people "strategizing" to convert you?
   - What are the points made about sin in the Jews for Jesus doctrinal statement? (Christianity believes that everyone sins [Eccesiastes 7:20] and that acceptance of the sacrifice of Jesus is needed to atone for these sins. Point out that Jews agree that people sin; however, repentance is accomplished through righting the wrong and prayer. Furthermore, from the *Akedah* story, Jews learn that human sacrifice is utterly forbidden.)

4. Analyze with the class a situation in which a Jew is being proselytized through the use of these texts. Ask students the following questions:
   - When a missionary of this type has been "primed" with literature like the literature we are reading, is he or she engaging in manipulation (of the Jewish person's emotions and thoughts)?
   - How might the Jewish person feel if the missionary is quoting from the Bible, using proof texts and arguments with which the Jewish person is unfamiliar? Why?
   - Are the missionary and the Jewish person on an equal footing?
   - Once the missionary creates a window of doubt or openness to the idea that Jesus is the Messiah, what then can he or she potentially do?
   - Christian missionary groups and Messianic Jewish groups claim that the Lubavitch sect of Chasidic Jews do the same as they. This, they argue, is why they should also be able to "convert" Jews. What is your response? (The Lubavitch leadership has responded that their interest is in making Jews more Jewish.)

- If all people have a right to free speech and individuals are free to believe as they choose, does the family of the Jewish person or the larger Jewish community have anything to fear by this individual's attempts to proselytize Jews? (Such proselytizing is a threat to those who are intellectually or emotionally vulnerable, especially new immigrants, the elderly, teens, and college students. Proselytizing thus takes unfair advantage of their situation. Jews for Jesus or Hebrew Christians also engage in religious defilement by reinterpreting Jewish symbols and history in a manner that strips Judaism of its intended meaning. Doing so is an affront to the integrity of Jewish tradition. Many mainstream Christian churches and communities condemn the efforts of these missionizing movements.)

5. Hand out copies of "Two Proof Texts Used by Missionaries" (pp. 93–94). On the handout are two texts often used by Christian missionaries. Read the texts aloud and use the article "Responding to Christian Recruiters" by Richard Birnholz (pp. 95–109) to explain how these texts are viewed from a Jewish perspective and a Christian missionary perspective. Have students list on the board or in their own notebooks the Jewish interpretations of these texts.

6. Have the students think about a missionary approaching a younger sibling or a friend. Ask the students if there are any elements of this situation, in addition to the ones discussed in class, that might make them upset. Have students write a letter to this younger sibling or friend, explaining their feelings and point of view.

Excerpts from

HOW TO WITNESS EFFECTIVELY TO THE JEWS

Moishe Rosen (of Jews for Jesus)

The Approach
"… form a friendship"

Use of Scripture
"We are not to use the Bible to smash the heads of our contenders, but rather we are to use it to pierce the heart …"

"You should be aware that your friend's Hebrew Bible will not always agree with your translation …"

Presentation of Gospel
"In presenting the Gospel to the Jewish person, we must … re-educate his thinking …"

Savior
"In the beginning of your discussion of Jesus Christ … do not feel that you must expound every aspect of the truth …"

"Avoid Christian jargon …": "Born again," "Blood of the Lamb," "Trinity," "Cross," "Church," "Christian," "Convert."

JEWS FOR JESUS
STRATEGY AND TACTICS

Jewish-Christian Music. Most Christian hymns and contemporary Christian songs are beautiful, worshipful, and a blessing to the church. However, they grate on Jewish sensibilities. For example, when a Jew hears "The Old Rugged Cross," his first response is, "That cross has meant the persecution of my people through the centuries."

The Lord has blessed us with a wealth of talented people. Among these are competent musicians, composers, and lyricists. These people have pooled their abilities to produce a fund of Jewish gospel music distinctly Jewish in flavor but proclaiming the gospel message. The melodies are reminiscent of Eastern European, American, and Israeli Jewish music. The lyrics for the most part are taken from Scripture. [ed. note—i.e., New Testament]

• • •

Mobile Evangelistic Teams. Our original music and drama is presented to the unbelieving world and to the church through our traveling teams—the Liberated Wailing Wall, the New Jerusalem Players, and Israelight. When our teams arrive in a city, they not only share in churches, Bible colleges, and seminaries, but they hold rallies on college campuses; they hand out broadsides and hold outdoor evangelistic meetings; they visit interested Jewish people; and they visit Jewish old-age homes and hospitals as they are permitted.

— Excerpts from pamphlet produced by Jews for Jesus

What evangelical Christians should know about

JEWS FOR JESUS
A CONFIDENTIAL REPORT

(not to be distributed to Non-Christians)

What We Believe: Doctrinal Statement

We define ourselves as evangelical fundamentalists and we seek the cooperation of individuals and Christian bodies meeting this description. We cannot allow ourselves to be committed to any single segment of the church. We believe *in affiliation with a local church* and in being *accountable to the church for service* and *discipline.* We will *uphold the local church* wherever we can.

We believe in the Divine Inspiration, infallibility, and authority of the Old and New Testament.

We believe in the Triune G-d and the deity of the Lord Jesus Christ, the only begotten Son of G-d.

We believe in His sacrificial atonement at Calvary, His bodily resurrection from the dead, and His premillenial Second Coming.

We believe that the New Birth by faith and obedience to Christ places each believer in the Body of Christ of which the local congregation is an expression.

We believe that it is necessary for the Christian to be separated from the worldly system of sin and resist the person of Satan.

Finally, we believe in the lost condition of every human being, whether Jew or gentile, who does not accept salvation by faith in Jesus Christ and, therefore, in the necessity of presenting the gospel to the Jews.

TWO PROOF TEXTS USED BY MISSIONARIES

Who would have believed our report? And to whom is the arm of the Lord revealed? For he grew up before him as a tender plant, and as a root out of a dry ground; he had no form nor comeliness, that we should look at him, and no countenance, that we should desire him. He was despised and rejected of men; a man of pains, and acquainted with sickness; and we hid as it were our faces from him; he was despised, and we esteemed him not. But in truth he has borne our sicknesses and endured our pains; yet we did esteem him stricken, smitten of God, and afflicted. But he was wounded because of our transgressions, bruised because of our iniquities; his sufferings were that we might have peace, and by his injury we are healed.

And we like sheep have gone astray; we have turned every one to his own way; and the Lord has caused the iniquity of us all to fall upon him. He was oppressed, but he humbled himself and opened not his mouth: as a lamb that is brought to the slaughter, and as a sheep before her shearers is dumb, so he did not open his mouth. By oppression and false judgment was he taken away; and of his generation who is considered? For he was cut off out of the land of the living, for the transgression of the people to whom the stroke was due. For they made his grave among the wicked, and his tomb among the rich; because he had done no violence, neither was any deceit in his mouth. But it pleased the Lord to crush him by disease; if his soul shall consider it a recompense for guilt, he shall see his seed, he shall prolong his days, and the purpose of the Lord shall prosper in his hand. He shall see the travail of his soul, he shall be sated with seeing; by his knowledge did My servant justify the Righteous One to the many, and did bear their iniquities. Surely I will give him a portion with the great, and he shall divide the spoil with the strong; because he has poured out his soul to death, and was numbered with transgressors;

but he bore the sin of many, and made intercession for the transgressors.

(Isaiah 53)

Therefore, the Lord Himself shall give you a sign: Behold, a young woman shall conceive and bear a son, and shall call his name Immanuel. He shall eat curd and honey when he knows how to refuse the evil and choose the good. For before the child knows how to refuse the evil and choose the good, the land before whose two kings you are in dread will be deserted.

(Isaiah 7:14–16)

RESPONDING TO CHRISTIAN RECRUITERS

[The following material is for optional use with Session 11 and is adapted from the teaching materials of Rabbi Richard Birnholz of Congregation Shaarai Zedek in Tampa, FL. Teachers may wish to use the material in a classroom dialogue, in role plays, or just as handouts for further reading. This material is reprinted with the kind permission of the author.]

Part 1—Is Jesus the Messiah? Dealing with the Distortions

The recruiter might say ...
The Jewish Bible (Old Testament) predicts that Jesus Christ would be the Messiah. Since the Old Testament is your Bible, surely you Jews must believe this to be true. After all, it's specifically written, so how can you deny it? In fact, given everything that is written and said about Jesus, how can you not believe in him?

Using as proof ...
A. Isaiah 7:14: "Therefore, the Lord Himself shall give you a sign: Behold, the virgin shall conceive and bear a son, and shall call his name Immanuel." (This predicts that Jesus was born as a sign of things to come. He was to be born of a virgin mother, a prophecy that is, in fact, fulfilled by Jesus. This belief is upheld in the New Testament Book of Matthew 1:23.)
B. Isaiah 53:2–5: "For he shot up right forth as a sapling, and as a root out of a dry ground; he had no form ... that we should look upon him.... He was despised, and forsaken of men.... He was despised; we esteemed him not. Surely our diseases he did bear and our pains he carried ... and with his stripes we were healed."
   • Isaiah 53:7: "He was oppressed, though he humbled himself and opened not his mouth."

- Isaiah 53:9: "And they made his grave with the wicked and with the rich his tomb."
- Isaiah 53:12: "... because he bared his soul unto death and was numbered with the transgressors; yet he bore the sin of many, and made intercession for the transgressors."

C. The Christian maintains that God showed his love for humanity by making the supreme sacrifice. He gave up his most beloved "son," Jesus, the one whom He made as a sign in Isaiah 7:14. The method and nature of this sacrifice is predicted in Isaiah 53. Jesus was despised and tortured and eventually killed by the people he tried to change (the Jews). He suffered because of what the Jews did to him, not because he himself did anything wrong. He was crucified together with thieves, yet because he was sacrificed in this way, he atoned for the basic sinfulness that is in all men. This is predicted in Isaiah 53, and Jesus, by the circumstances of his life, fulfilled the prophecy. These are only two of more than three hundred such prophecies in the Bible.

Background ...

A. Isaiah 7:14: This passage was written seven hundred years before Jesus. It was spoken by the prophet Isaiah, who was the foreign-policy advisor to Ahaz, the king of Judah. Ahaz faced a difficult situation: The kings of Israel and Syria to the north wanted him to join them in a military alliance against Assyria, a threatening power in the east. Ahaz refused, so the two kings laid siege to Jerusalem. As the pressure grew greater, Ahaz decided to ask Assyria for help. But Isaiah disagreed with this plan, fearing it would make Judah even more obligated to the hated Assyrian giant. Ahaz, however, would not listen. So Isaiah said, "God will send you a sign telling you to remain completely neutral and have faith that God will protect you in this neutrality. The sign is, 'Behold, *the* young woman will conceive and bear a son, and shall call his name Immanuel.'"

Notice, the prophecy speaks about *the* young woman, not just *a* young woman. It, therefore, had to refer to someone the king knew well, possibly someone who lived close to the king so that as he watched the child mature, the king would be reminded daily of the prophet's words. So it either referred to Ahaz's queen or, even more likely, Isaiah's wife, whose other two children also bore symbolic names. The new child would be a faithful descendant of David, true to *Adonai*. Through him, "God would be with us" (which is what the Hebrew word "Immanuel" means).

Note that:
- Jesus is never mentioned.
- Signs of this kind were a common element of religious predictions of that day.
- The Hebrew version of the young woman is *Almah*. This does not mean a virgin. The word was mistranslated by the Greeks in their version. Today many Christian translations of the Bible have changed the translation back to a young woman rather than virgin.
- It is likely that the men who wrote the story of Jesus in the New Testament formed the "facts" of his life to correspond with this description of a son so that it looks as though a prediction has been fulfilled. Many Christian scholars even admit to this today.

B. Isaiah 53: The individual who is the suffering servant of God is described elsewhere in the Bible as well. Generally the servant is "the People Israel" because all Israelites are supposed to serve God by spreading God's moral law throughout the world. However, in this case the servant suffers for sins not of his own making. There is no concept of this in Judaism. If you suffer it is because you have sinned. Who, then, is this suffering servant of God? It is probably the prophet Isaiah himself. He was hated and despised for making the people feel uncomfortable because he told them of their immoral acts. Yet because he was willing to endure suffering, they finally came to realize that he was right.

C. Furthermore, according to Judaism, *one cannot atone for the sins of another.* Individual Jews are always responsible for their own wrongdoing. The sinner must repent before God forgives. So Jesus could not atone for us. Thus the suffering servant in Isaiah was not a prediction of Jesus because:

- It doesn't mention Jesus.
- No Messiah would atone for a wrongdoer in Judaism.
- The second Isaiah, who wrote this passage, lived at least 550 years before Jesus and had no idea what would happen that far ahead of time.
- The facts in the passage make more sense when applied to Isaiah and his work.

The Bible does tell about the coming of a Messiah who would be sent by God. But this Messiah was never supposed to be Divine. Some translations of Isaiah, chapter 9, may describe the Messiah figure as "Mighty God," but the phrase more accurately should be translated as "God-like hero." This translation is reinforced by Isaiah, chapter 11, which describes this Messiah as follows: "And his delight shall be in the fear of the Lord. He shall not judge by what his eyes see or decide by what his ears hear." You will note that he is not described as *Adonai* but that his delight shall be in the fear of the Lord, and it was in this way he was to be exceptional. He was also expected to be special in that with his coming he would bring everlasting peace and justice to the Jewish people and the world, just as King David had done in an earlier age. (Isaiah 2:4: "... and they shall beat their swords into plowshares and their spears into pruning-hooks; nation shall not lift up sword against nation, neither shall they learn war any more."

Jesus, however, as described by basic Christian theology, does not fit these Jewish expectations for the Messiah because:

- Jesus became Divine.
- Peace did not come to the Jews when Jesus arose. In fact, only more persecution has followed since then, much be-

cause of Christian teachings. The early Christians knew this and so conceived the idea of the Second Coming of Jesus in the future. His first appearance was the time of his crucifixion. Judaism, however, never mentioned a Second Coming.

You may answer the recruiter by saying …

1. I will accept your interpretation that Jesus is the son in Isaiah 7:14 or the servant in Isaiah, chapter 53, if you can show me where Jesus' name is written in these verses or anywhere else in the Jewish Bible. If the recruiter tries to say that the actual name of Jesus linked to this prophecy is in the New Testament, remind him that he said the prediction was in the Jewish Bible. *Refuse to answer any more charges until this one is answered.* If the recruiter tries to change the subject, re-ask the question again and again until he gives in or goes away.

OR

I believe that your interpretation of the Bible is true for you just as mine is true for me. But since they are different, let's just agree to respect our differences and talk about something else.

2. When the recruiter says, "Given all that is written and said about Jesus, how can you not accept him?" answer, "Given everything that is written about Buddha, how can you not accept him?"

3. A number of well-known Christian scholars, including Norman K. Gottwald, author of *A Light to the Nations,* and B. W. Anderson, author of *Understanding the Old Testament,* seriously question whether Jesus could have been the messianic figure referred to in Isaiah 7:14 and 53. If you have an opportunity to read this material and feel you understand it and can present it effectively, then by all means do so. Nothing is more devastating than forcing a recruiter to defend his stance against another Christian—especially when that Christian is a recognized scholar. But remember, take this approach only if you can handle the material with ease.

General strategy to answer any fundamentalist who says that his or her interpretation of the Bible is the only true one ...

Whether the fundamentalist quotes Isaiah or any other Bible text to prove that Jesus' coming is predicted in the Jewish Bible, you might want to use the following statement: "If there were just one correct understanding of God's written word in the Bible, then we wouldn't have fifteen or more Christian denominations differing in opinion over what the Bible says. Obviously, then, no individual's or group's interpretation of the Bible can be the *only* correct one, yours included."

After stating this, turn and walk away.

Part 2—Is Judaism a Cold Religion of Harsh Law?

The recruiter might say ...
Judaism is a religion of harsh law. The Jewish God is a mean and demanding one. Christianity, on the other hand, is a religion of love because Jesus is a living symbol of the warmth and mercy from God.

Using as proof ...
Paul of Tarsus, the Christian who first formalized Christian thought, took a look at Jewish law, especially Deuteronomy 27:15–27. This passage lists eleven basic ethical obligations, including prohibitions against violence, bribery, oppression of the weak, etc. At the end of the passage it says, "Cursed be the one who does not maintain all the words of this Torah, to do them."

Paul explained that this shows the strictness of Judaism. You can't break one law. And if you do, you are punished severely. Surely, says Paul, everyone will violate at least one law; therefore, anyone who tries to obey the Jewish God is cursed and works under a terrible burden. Christianity, on the other hand, believes that God loves all those who believe in Jesus, even if they sometimes do wrong. Everyone is going to sin at some point, and God understands this. God forgives by God's sheer grace because Jesus already died for the sins we will commit.

Background ...
This charge is a cruel one, based on misunderstanding and bad will. When Deuteronomy 27 talks about strict punishment for failing to keep the law, it is referring specifically to the eleven prohibitions stated therein. It is unfair, then, to apply this harsh curse to all the laws in the Torah. Furthermore, Judaism has always allowed the Jew who breaks the law to repent. That is why we have Rosh Hashanah and Yom Kippur. On Rosh Hashanah we remember our failings from the past year, and on Yom Kippur we come before God to say, "I'm sorry. I'll change my ways." And

according to our tradition, God forgives us and says, "Try again."

Jewish law is also humane. It tells us we *must* do things, but what is it we must do? We must help the poor, the sick, the blind, the stranger, even the donkey that has fallen under its load. Could a mean God make such laws?

It is true Judaism has laws, but then we all need laws to help us know where to go in our lives. Without a red light, I might accidentally run into another car. God gives us laws *because* God loves us, because God wants us to get along. And we believe God will always forgive us when we break the laws as long as we are sincere in our repentance and work to correct our mistakes.

Jesus himself, in fact, said that we must obey the law. To his early disciples he said, "I tell you solemnly, till heaven and earth disappear, not one dot, not one little stroke, shall disappear from the law. Therefore, the man who infringes even the least of these commandments and teaches others to do the same will be considered least in the kingdom of heaven." (Matthew 5:17–19)

So, when you are told that Judaism is a religion of strict law and that Christianity is better because it is a religion of love, **you may say ...**

1. I too believe Jesus was probably a man who loved all people for what they were and not for what they might become. So I think even Jesus would accept me exactly as I am.

OR

2. Jesus taught: "Do unto others as you would have them do unto you." You wouldn't want anyone trying to convert you, so please don't try to convert me.

3. You say Judaism is a religion of strict law, while Jesus promises forgiveness? Isn't your one and only law that you have to believe in Jesus to be saved and that failure dooms you to hell? This law and punishment seems much harsher to me than any in Judaism. I guess we just have different ways of looking at things.

Part 3—Do Jews Have to Believe in Jesus to Become Complete or Fulfilled Jews?

The recruiter might say ...

At first the Jews *were* God's chosen people. God chose them to bear God's word. God used the prophets to carry the Divine message. But somehow the Jews faltered in their responsibility, and God made a new covenant (New Testament) with a new people—the Christians—and thus God's greatest prophet Jesus. *Christianity, then, is the fulfillment of Judaism. Christianity completes what Judaism fails to do. Christianity is consequently the truest religion of all.* To really be a Jew, you have to believe in Jesus; otherwise you are not a complete Jew.

Using as proof ...

God elects certain prophets to teach the Divine word. God began with Abraham and then used Isaac, Jacob, and Moses. The prophets, like Isaiah and Jeremiah, continued to hear and speak God's message, and with their passing Jesus continued to do this work. Jesus is obviously a prophet because he received a call to do his work just as others did before him. He is also given the power to work miracles like Moses. He was the last of the great prophets, and so the religion he represents, Christianity, is obviously the most complete of all religions.

Background ...

In Judaism we don't say there is only one true or complete religion in the world because we believe there is more than one acceptable religious avenue to God. Therefore, we say that as long as the other religions ask their members to follow the basic moral laws as we know them (such as the Ten Commandments), we consider those religions valid.

Considering Christianity, then, to be the best or most complete religion because it came last is as foolish as regarding Judaism as the best religion because it came first. Indeed, there are those

Jews who hold that Christianity is a watering down of true Judaism, which Christianity tried to steal away from us. But this argument is no fairer than the Christian one that last is best.

We must also remember that Jesus was born a Jew and died a Jew and that most of his New Testament teachings are basic Jewish concepts. Surely this must speak for Jesus' favorable feelings about the completeness of Judaism. Would he have been a Jew if Judaism hadn't met his religious needs?

What Judaism requires is that the Jew keep the ethical laws and, depending on whether one is Reform, Conservative, or Orthodox, some or all of the ritual laws. This is what God expects of us under God's covenantal agreement with us. Nowhere in the Bible are we told we must believe in Jesus to be complete Jews.

When a recruiter says that Christianity is the religion that makes Judaism complete, **you may answer ...**

1. Did you know that Jesus was born a Jew and died a Jew and taught Judaism to his followers? If Judaism was good enough for Jesus it's good enough for me. (Then walk away.)

OR

2. I know a lot of Jews who say that Christianity is nothing but a watered-down form of Judaism designed to appeal to pagans living in Jesus' time, and that if one really wants a pure version of the Hebraic faith he can get it only in Judaism. But I know that this is just as unfair as saying that Judaism needs Jesus to make it complete.

Part 4—Is the Jew Doomed to Eternal Damnation?

The recruiter might say ...
Since Jews don't believe in Jesus as the Messiah, they will not be forgiven for their sins. Therefore, they will go to hell.

Using as proof ...
Humanity is basically sinful because of what Adam and Eve did in the garden. When they sinned, they were told God would punish them by making Adam work for a living and by giving Eve pain in childbirth. Furthermore, God said that all men and women would inherit this punishment, and that's why all men and women face these difficulties today. All of us, then, have been born with Adam and Eve's sinfulness, and that's why we do so many immoral things. And we can never shake off this sinfulness no matter how hard we try or how much we repent. Jesus, however, is our savior. He saves us from the doom that is unavoidable because he died for our sins on the cross. He was God's gift to us. By offering him as a sacrifice, God gave us a way to wash away our sins. Indeed, this is the only kind of atonement that would work because the atonement must come through a blood offering. In Leviticus 17:11, it says, "The life of the flesh is in the *blood*, and I have given it to you upon the altar to make an atonement for your souls; for it is the *blood* that maketh atonement for the soul." In biblical times the Jews knew they were supposed to slaughter animals and dash their blood around in order to be forgiven. But in the time of Jesus, humanity came to realize that Jesus was the sacrifice of sacrifices. Once God had given us Jesus on the cross, humanity only needed to acknowledge Jesus and all sins would be forgiven.

However, those who do not believe that Jesus was the Messiah who died for our sins as predicted in Isaiah 53 will burn in hell. This is why Christian recruiters pray for us; they pray that we will accept Jesus as our savior before we die and are punished in the afterlife with the fires of hell.

Background ...

1. Jews do not believe that humanity inherited Adam and Eve's sinfulness. Jews believe that we inherited the punishment of work and pain in childbirth, but this is different from inheriting the state of sinfulness. The Jew, in fact, interprets the Adam and Eve narrative to mean that God gave the couple the freedom to choose: They could either eat the apple or leave it. Judaism teaches that everyone chooses how to behave—righteously (by keeping God's laws) or sinfully (by breaking God's laws), and it's up to the individual to decide which path to follow. If you choose to act sinfully you are punished, but you also have the opportunity, according to rabbinical teaching, to ask God for forgiveness, change your ways, and thus be forgiven. So even if you do sin, you are not doomed forever.

2. Jews believe that human sacrifices have no place in our faith. This is the message of the story of the binding of Isaac. Abraham was about to imitate his Canaanite neighbors by sacrificing his most beloved son to show his faith in God, but the Jewish God stopped him and said, "No, don't do it." Jews do not believe in human sacrifice. In the years just before the Second Temple was destroyed, even animal blood sacrifices ended, and the rabbis explained that what God wanted was broken hearts instead of broken, bloody bodies. God wants humanity to say, "I'm sorry, and I'll change." God doesn't want us to believe in or participate in a blood offering. Ultimately, God wants us to change our ways instead.

3. Furthermore, Jews believe that no one can atone for them. All people must atone for themselves. The priests used to atone for us by offering our sacrifices to God, but when the Temple was destroyed, so was the priesthood. After that, Jews were expected to say "I'm sorry" themselves. Belief in Jesus cannot do it for us.

When a recruiter claims that Jews are doomed to hell because they don't believe in Jesus, **you may say ...**

1. Thank you for being concerned about me. (Then walk away. You must walk away; otherwise this strategy will not work. If you stay and argue, the recruiter will not understand that you mean it when you say that you are glad he or she is concerned about you. By walking away and refusing to say anything further, you are, in a nice way, asking the recruiter to mind his or her own business. So be sure to walk away at once and don't even look back.)

OR

2. If belief in Jesus makes your religion complete, that's great, but I feel my religion is complete without it. But thank you for being so concerned anyway. (Then walk away.)

OR

3. Listen, nobody really knows what happens after death. No one has ever come back to tell us. Do you remember what it was like before you were born? Of course you don't. Neither do you know what life will be like after death. *That's why I worry about the way I act here and now.* I know that's what God expects of me.

Part 5—Are Jews Really Christ-Killers?

The recruiter might say ...
You Jews killed Christ and that's why your people have to suffer so much persecution: God is punishing you.

Recruiters may operate **under the assumption that ...**
Jews killed Jesus, and because of this terrible murder, God has punished the Jew throughout Jewish history. It's because the Jews killed Jesus that six million Jews were gassed and cremated in Nazi camps and thousands were burned at the stake during the Spanish Inquisition. That's why Jews always suffer: because they killed Christ and they have refused to accept and love him.

Background ...
The Jews didn't kill Jesus. The Romans did. Crucifixion was a Roman method of execution, not a Jewish one. Furthermore, the Jewish Sanhedrin would not have met at night or on the eve of Passover (it is forbidden by Jewish law to meet on the eve of a holy day or the Sabbath), nor would it have met in the house of a high priest (it would have met only in the Chamber of Hewn Stone). Therefore, the Sanhedrin that tried Jesus was one of Roman making. It was not Jewish.

The New Testament is not even clear about exactly what happened. Each of the four gospels—Matthew, Mark, Luke, and John—has a different version of the crucifixion. But what does appear probable from all the gospels is that Jesus was executed by the Romans for treason because he was a revolutionary who was trying to free Israel from Roman oppression.

When the recruiter says, "You Jews are Christ-killers and have suffered because God is punishing you for it," **you may answer ...**

I know you have been taught this belief, but it isn't true and it is a terrible thing to say. Just think about it: Would Jesus, who taught people to "love thy neighbor as thyself," have approved of Jewish persecution in his name? If you believe that, I may have a better understanding of Jesus than you do.

SESSION 12

Concluding Activity
Include or Exclude Jews Involved in Cults from Synagogue and Community Membership?

Objective

To give students an opportunity to articulate some of the concerns, opinions, and values they have learned from their study of cults.

Materials

Handout: "Cult Members Apply for Synagogue Membership: An Outline for a Board Meeting at Congregation X" (pp. 112–113).

Activities

1. Have the students role-play or dramatize a synagogue board meeting using the situation, cast of characters, and meeting procedure outlined in the following handout. Select a student to write the minutes of the meeting on the board, outlining the different issues and the board's position.

2. Have the class discuss the following:
   - Can the synagogue exclude the family from Temple membership? Should it? And if so, on what grounds?
   - What is the synagogue's institutional and religious rationale for this position?

- Are there precedents (legal or otherwise) for this position?
- Has this happened in any other synagogues?
- Is this an issue of First Amendment rights?

3. Design a strategy with students for use by the congregation in pursuing possible responses. Is there more than one viable response?

CULT MEMBERS APPLY FOR SYNAGOGUE MEMBERSHIP AN OUTLINE FOR A BOARD MEETING AT CONGREGATION X

SITUATION

A middle-aged couple has just joined the congregation and enrolled its two children (ages 10 and 12) in the religious school. Several weeks after the couple's application for membership was accepted, the couple shared with several other congregants that it was affiliated with a particular political organization. This organization had a very negative reputation; it was considered a political cult. The couple had no hesitation sharing this information and even offered to pass on some literature to congregants. Both also suggested that at some point they put together a program at the synagogue for other members who might be interested in learning more about their organization. The congregants with whom the couple had shared this information became quite concerned and notified the rabbi and the congregation president. The two agreed to call a closed-session board meeting to discuss the situation.

CHARACTERS

The rabbi, **Janet Weiss**, has served in a congregational setting for five years. She has been at this congregation one year and is preparing to renegotiate her contract.

The temple president, **Jeffrey Klein**, is a junior-executive type in his late 40s. He is concerned primarily with the image of the congregation and its potential long-term growth.

The ex-president, **Sarah Lehr**, is a longtime member of the congregation, who happens to be politically conservative.

Richard Feldstein is a corporate attorney in his late 30s, who specializes in real estate and tax law.

Harriet Blum is a social worker in her 50s. She is the divorced mother of two college students.

Frieda Millstein is a psychologist, with very liberal leanings. She is an outspoken woman, also in her 50s, who was very active during the 1960s in antiwar protests.

Richard Block is a retired businessman and member of the congregation for 40 years. He is also a big financial contributor.

Susan Freeling is a dance instructor at a local college. She is quiet and hardworking. She is also a Jew-by-Choice and the mother of three young children (ages 6, 9, 12) in religious school.

Sam Tattlebaum is a retired physician, who claims to be "not religious." His grandchildren are in religious school; the oldest one is about to become a bat mitzvah. His son, who had been involved in the Moonies for several years, had to be "kidnapped" from the organization. He received extensive counseling following his departure from the Moonies but still has many personal problems.

Miriam Rabinowitz is a public high school teacher. She is into New Age ideas, though she teaches in the religious school.

Harold Sachs is an unmarried optometrist, who is relatively new to the congregation. He left a neighboring congregation five years ago because of politics.

THE MEETING

1. Have each student play one of the board members of Congregation X.
2. Have the temple president call the meeting to order and address the board.
3. The student playing the rabbi should then outline the issues involved, such as the concerns of the various congregants, legal considerations, and basic ideological question of what is the right or wrong thing to do.
4. Have the rabbi open the meeting.
5. Ask the board members to discuss their concerns.
6. When the meeting is done, have the temple president call a vote on whether the couple can retain its membership.
7. Count up the votes and then ask students to explain outside of their characters what they think should be done.

Appendix I

Session 1: Introduction to the Issues

Classroom Materials

The Wave, a film by Embassy Productions, 46 minutes. *The Wave* is available from your local Board of Jewish Education; the Simon Wiesenthal Center, 9760 West Pico Boulevard, Yeshiva University of Los Angeles, Los Angeles, CA 90035; and Films, Inc./Education, 5547 North Ravenswood Avenue, Chicago, IL 60640-1199, 312-878-2600 (Illinois) or 800-323-4222 (contact: Chuck Fuller, ext. 388). Purchase price: $79/video or $750/film. Rental rate: $75/day.

Session 2: The Characteristics of a Cult

Classroom Materials

Information packets containing 40–60 pages of journal, magazine, and newspaper articles on those groups listed in Activity 2 (p. 15) and marked with an asterisk (*). The packet is available for approximately $10 each from the American Family Foundation (AFF), c/o International Cult Education Program, P.O. Box 1232, Gracie Station, New York, NY 10028, 212-533-5420, Fax: 212-533-0538.

Resources

Andres, Rachel, and James R. Lane, eds. "Are Destructive Cults Physically Dangerous?" in *Cults and Consequences: The Definitive Hand-*

book. Los Angeles: Commission on Cults and Missionaries of the Jewish Federation Council of Greater Los Angeles, 1988.

Andron, Sandy. *Cultivating Cult-Evading*. Miami: Central Agency for Jewish Education, 1983.

Rudin, Marcia R. *Too Good to Be True: Resisting Cults and Psychological Manipulation, A Lesson Plan for Middle Schools and High Schools*. New York: International Cult Education Program, 1992.

Session 3: Comparing Cults to Mainstream Religions

Classroom Materials
Neusner, Jacob, ed. *World Religions in America*. Louisville: Westminster/Sam Knox Press, 1994. (Suggestions: "Protestant Christianity in the World and in America" by Martin E. Marty, pp. 33–68; "The Catholics in the World and in America" by Andrew M. Greeley, pp. 93–110; "Judaism in the World and in America" by Jacob Neusner, pp. 151–176; "Buddhism in the World and in America" by Malcolm David Eckel, pp. 203–218; "Islam in the World and in America" by Sam L. Esposito, pp. 243–258.)

Resource
Andron, Sandy. *Cultivating Cult-Evading*. (See Session 2 above.)

Session 4: Jewish Ideals and Values That Challenge Cults

Classroom Materials
Tanach.

Resources
UAHC Department of Interreligious Affairs. *Missionary and Cult Movements: A Mini-Course for Upper Grades in Religious Schools*. New York: UAHC, 1982.

Plaut, W. Gunter, ed. *The Torah: A Modern Commentary*. New York: UAHC Press, 1981.

Session 5: Destructive Versus Nondestructive Cults

Resources
Hassan, Steven. *Combatting Cult Mind Control*. Rochester, VT: Park Street Press, 1988.

Langone, Michael D., ed. *Recovery from Cults*. New York: W. W. Norton, 1993.

Langone, Michael D., and Linda O. Blood. *Satanism and Occult-Related Violence: What You Should Know*. Weston, MA: American Family Foundation, 1990.

Session 6: Why Do People Join Cults?

Classroom Materials

Ticket to Heaven, an R. L. Thomas Film, Inc., 107 minutes. *Ticket to Heaven* is available from local Boards of Jewish Education. Blockbuster Video will special order it for a cost of approximately $79.

Session 7: Why Jews Join Cults

Classroom Materials:

You Can Go Home Again, a video production of the UAHC TV & Film Institute, 47 minutes. *You Can Go Home Again* is available from the UAHC, No. 586860, $19.95. Call the UAHC Press Order Department, 212-650-4121 (9:00 A.M.–5:00 P.M. E.S.T.) or 212-650-4119 (24-hour fax number).

Resource

Kametz, Roger. *The Jew in the Lotus: A Poet's Rediscovery of Jewish Identity in Buddhist India*. San Francisco: Harper & Row, 1994.

Session 8: Who Recruits and Why?

Classroom Materials

Hassan, Steven. *Combatting Cult Mind Control.* (See Session 5 above.)
Information packets from the American Family Foundation. (See Session 2 above.)

Session 9: Techniques of Recruitment

Classroom Materials

Cults: Saying 'No' Under Pressure, a film by the International Cult Education Program and the InService Videotape Network of the National Association of Secondary School Principals, 25 minutes. Produced by

Instructivision, Inc., and narrated by Charlton Heston. Available for purchase from International Cult Education Program, P. O. Box 1232, Gracie Station, New York, NY 10028, 212-533-5420, Fax: 212-533-0538. $75 or $59 for members, plus $2.50/tape for postage and handling, $5/tape for Canadian and overseas orders.

Session 10: The Development of the Messianic Idea and the Jewish Position on Jesus

Resource

UAHC Department of Interreligious Affairs. *Missionary and Cult Movements: A Mini-Course for Upper Grades in Religious Schools.* (See Session 4 above.)

Session 11: How to Respond to Christian Missionaries and the Proof Texts They Use

Classroom Materials

Jewish Community Task Force on Missionary Activities of the Synagogue Council of Massachusetts. *Refuting Christian Missionaries: Teaching Materials and Facilitator's Guide.* Boston: Synagogue Council of Massachusetts, n.d.

Birnholz, Richard. "Responding to Christian Recruiters." Unpublished manuscript.

Appendix II

Cult-Awareness Organizations

American Family Foundation (AFF), c/o International Cult Education Program, P.O. Box 1232, Gracie Station, New York, NY 10028, 212-533-5420, Fax: 212-533-0538.

Center on Destructive Cultism, P.O. Box 336, 413 Boston Post Road, Weston, MA 02193.

Citizen's Freedom Foundation, P.O. Box 86, Hannacroix, NY 12087.

Council on Mind Abuse, Box 575, Station 2, Toronto, Ontario, CANADA M5N 2Z6.

Cult Awareness Network, 2421 West Pratt Boulevard, Suite 1173, Chicago, IL 60645, 312-267-7777.

Cult Clinic, Jewish Family Service of Los Angeles, 6505 Wilshire Boulevard, Suite 608, Los Angeles, CA 90048, 213-852-1234, ext. 1650.

Cult Clinic/Hot Line, Jewish Board of Family and Children's Services, 1651 Third Avenue, New York, NY 10028, 212-860-8533.

Ex-Moon, Inc., Suite 1010, 1812 I Street NW, Washington, DC 20006.

FOCUS (Former Cultists Support Network), c/o Cult Awareness Network (CAN), 2421 West Pratt Boulevard, Suite 1173, Chicago, IL 60645, 312-267-7777. Contact: Marty Butz.

Simon Wiesenthal Center, 9760 West Pico Boulevard, Yeshiva University of Los Angeles, Los Angeles, CA 90035.

Spiritual Counterfeits Project, P.O. Box 4308, Berkeley, CA 94704, 415-524-9534.

Task Force on Missionaries and Cults, Jewish Community Relations Council (JCRC) of New York, 711 Third Avenue, 12th Floor, New York, NY 10017, 212-983-4800.

DATE DUE			

SPEIZMAN JEWISH LIBRARY

5007 PROVIDENCE ROAD

CHARLOTTE, NC 28226

(704) 944-6763